W. H. Jackson

The Texas stock directory;

Or, Book of marks and brands. In a series of volumes designed to embrace the entire State - Vol. 1

W. H. Jackson

The Texas stock directory;
Or, Book of marks and brands. In a series of volumes designed to embrace the entire State - Vol. 1

ISBN/EAN: 9783337730567

Printed in Europe, USA, Canada, Australia, Japan

Cover: Foto ©ninafisch / pixelio.de

More available books at **www.hansebooks.com**

THE

Texas Stock Directory,

OR

BOOK OF MARKS AND BRANDS.

IN A SERIES OF VOLUMES
DESIGNED TO EMBRACE THE ENTIRE STATE.

BY

W. H. JACKSON,
    Stockraiser of Bexar County,

S. A. LONG,
    Stockraiser of Medina County.

Volume I.

SAN ANTONIO:
PRINTED AT THE HERALD OFFICE,
1865.

PREFACE.

In bringing before the public this the first Volume of the Stock Directory or Brand Book, we deem that a few words are called for by way of apology. Circumstances over which we have had no control have retarded the publication of the work several months beyond what was at first anticipated. We presume that we need hardly say that those hindering circumstances grew out of the war by which our country has been so fearfully convulsed up to within a very short period. And while it is true that to this cause is mainly attributable the delay in the appearance of our work, there were found other difficulties which had to be overcome, not the least of which was found in the apathy and want of faith in the utility of the work on the part of those interested in it. Perhaps this should cause us little surprise, for it not unfrequently happens that those enterprizes redounding most to the benefit of the public, are slowest in being appreciated. We now feel, however, that the Rubicon has been passed, and if, with the assistance of this work, Stock-raising does not become more profitable, and the calling more reputable, we shall frankly acknowledge our disappointment.

The utility of such a work as this is too evident to require much remark, since it is a well known fact, that every neighborhood has within its bounds more or less animals bearing brands unknown to the citizens thereof. By means of this book the ownership of these strays is made known and the animals recovered.

The present system of stock-raising in Texas is not only unprofitable to a large proportion of those engaged therein, but is gradually becoming, in many localities, to a considerable degree disreputable. This, in common with the mass of our fellow-stockraisers, we are sorry to see and be compelled to admit. Pastoral life is almost as ancient as the world itself. Healthy, to a considerable degree pleasant, it could, in many portions of our State be made highly profitable according to the capital invested; *provided*, we would all obey the Scriptural injunction, "*Do unto others as we would that they should do unto us.*"

In order to make this work useful in restoring lost Stock to their rightful owners two things are essential: In the first place, when stock is sold it should be invariably contrabranded. Second, when strange animals to the range are discovered, every stock-raiser should make it his duty to examine the Directory, ascertain to whom the animal or animals belong, and give such information as will lead to the recovery of the same. If this should be done, thousands of animals will be restored to their owners, that would otherwise be a permanent loss. To a good man, the consciousness of having performed an act of kindness towards his fellow man, would be a sufficient reward, even though he should not be the recipient of any other, which would not often occur· for we are of those who believe that there few persons who would not cheerfully give remuneration in some way for information leading to the recovery of their lost stock.

The Publishers embrace the occasion to say that they expect to proceed with the Second Volume (which will embrace the territory lying between the Guadalupe and the Colorado) at an early day, and hope those who wish to have their Brands inserted will send them forward at once.   PUBLISHERS.

MARKS AND BRANDS.

NOTE OF EXPLANATION.

Swallow-fork in left ear,   Crop off right,

Split in left ear,   Crop and Under Bit,

Two Upper Bits,   Under half Crop,

Upper Slope,   Under Slope,

Ear Bob,   Crop and Upper Half Crop,

A Star (*) placed before a brand or mark denotes that it is not now used.

UVALDE CO.—UVALDE P. O.

W. C. Adams,   OT

do.   LOT

P. T. & M. V. Adams,   OUR

do.   *UR

UVALDE COUNTY.

D. G. Adams,	OUL	
do.	WD	
do.	PH	
do.	IES	
	* * * *	
E. A. Bates,	☉	
J. L. C. Boon,	⋂	
G. W. Brown,	⍏	
David Cook,	COOK	
do.	EJ	
W. T. Cook,	TC	
J. M. Adams,	PD	*

UVALDE COUNTY. 7

John C. Crawford,	M ⊂⊃	*⊂⊃
do.	NUN	⊂⊃
do.	RN	⊂⊃
do.	NG	⊂⊃
do.	↺	⊂⊃
do.	Ⓕ	⊂⊃
do.	Ⓐ	⊂⊃
do.	15 ⊂⊃	⊂⊃
do.	2	⊂⊃
do.	♡	⊂⊃
do.	51	⊂⊃
Dan. Davis,	⌐|	⊂⊃

UVALDE COUNTY.

Name	Brand	Marks
J. W. Cummings,	C	
do.	C (with bar over)	
E. U. Dale,	ED	
H. W. Griner,	FS	
do.	*H	
N. J. Griner,	NJ	
A. J. Griner,	H	
H. C. Griner,	HU	
James Hughs,	HS (reversed S)	
T. H. Harrison,	IX	
do.	(F)	
T. N. McKinney,	CC	

UVALDE CORNTY. 9

Tho's Hannahan,	TH	
do.	th	
W. B. Lease,	)-(	
do.	A	
D. T. Richeson,	R	
W. F. Smith,	IOI	
do.	WFS	
W. L. Shores,	WS	
N. L. Stratton,	S	
do.	NLS	
T. M. Vanpelt,	TE	
G. W. Wall,	WAL	

UVALDE COUNTY.

D. D. Wall,	A	
E. D. Westfall,	W	
T. Watkins,	ħ	
James H. Taylor,	T	
do.	P	
W. M. Reynolds,	SIX	
Reynolds & Adams,	RUN	
W. B. Bowles,	DOK	
do.	WT	
W. M. Evans,	WE	
J. Q. Dougherty,	D	
S. R. Miller,	JC	

	UVALDE COUNTY.	11
J. B Sanders,	B S	
J. T. McKinney,	JE	
Eliza C. McKinney,	96	
J. E. McKinney.	L O	
Jessie Lewis,	J	
W. M. Evans,	W E	
do	⌒	
Lewis O'Gi,	O L	
Mary Hannahan,	T H	
John Hill,	H I L	
	SABINAL P. O.	
J. G. Brown,	J O	

UVALDE COUNTY.

W. A. Brown,	3C	⊖⊖	⋑⋐
do.	Ⓑ		⊖⊖
Aaron Anglin,	OA		⊂⊃
do	JB		⊂⊃
Warren Allen,	WA		⊖⊖
do.	U [On Shoulder.]		⊖⊖
Hamner's Heirs	U [On Hip.]		⊖⊖
Miss Virginia Allen,	TXS		⊖⊖
J. H. Crane	HC		⊂⊃
W. A. Crane,	⊕ ⋹⋺	*	⋑⋐ ⋑⋐
John Davenport,	JD		⊖⋐

UVADE COUNTY. 13

Greenville Bowls,	SAL	
do.	ST	
do.	SIS	
do.	B	
do.	* +	
Mrs. Mary Davenport,	JD	
do.	I JD	
L. C. Davenport,	XL	
do.	* Ⓙ	
7. A. Davenport,	Ⓙ	*
A. B. Dillard,	AD	
Allen Dillard,	D	

UVALDE COUNTY.

Name	Brand	Mark
Joseph Dillard,	D	
L. Fleming,	LET	
O. D. Fleming,	T (with arc)	
Joel D. Fenly,	AB	
John. M. Fenly,	F	
Joel C. Fenly,	F	
James M. Fenly,	F	
C. D. Fenly,	FLE	
W. S. Hiler,	ZH	
do.	BE	
do.	5	
L. C. Kelley,	9K	

UVALDE COUNTY. 15

John Kennedy,	TK	
do.	⚓	
do.	*GK	
do.	3O	
N. M. C. Leakey,	JL	
John Leakey,	JH	
G. T. Nimmo,	O✗S	
W. H. Pulliam,	OX	
G. W. Patterson, sen.,	GP	
John C. Patterson,	JP	
G. W. Patterson, jun.,	P A T	
do.	*P	

UVALDE COUNTY.

Name	Brand	Mark
W. B. Patterson,	BIL	⊂⊃
G. R. Patterson,	N	⊂⊃
N. M. C. Patterson,	9	⊂⊃
J. W. Patterson,	AIL	⊂⊃
J. J. H. Patterson,	JIL	⊂⊃
F. Rooney,	UI	⊖
G. L. Snow,	E	⊕⊗
B. F. Taylor,	F̂ ⊂⊃	⊖
do.	BT	⊂⊃
B. W. Taylor,	F̂ ⊂⊃	⊖
do.	DO	⊂⊃
T. E. Taylor,	LE	⊂⊃

UVALDE COUNTY.

Name	Brand	Mark
T. E. Taylor,	WW	
do.	*E	
do.	*ħ	
R. M. Ware,	R	
Miss. S. T. Ware,	WW	
Wilson O'Brion,	℃	
Esther J. Norton,	m	
Mrs. E. Robinson,	ER	
John C. Ware,	JW	
Silas Webster,	2	
J. B. Davenport,	JB	

UVALDE COUNTY.

Name	Brand	Mark
C. C McKinney,	(I)	
W. M. Peppers	EP	
P. J. Dawson,	♃P	
B. A. Pulliam,	U V	
E. A. Nimmo,	N	

Eagle Pass P. O.

Name	Brand	Mark
Ben. Thomas,	ƀ	
Penelope Thomas,	ƀ	
Laura Thomas,	◇	
Benj. Thomas,	⇧	
Penelope Thomas,	♃	

DAWSON COUNTY.

Name	Brand	Mark
Wm. S. Thomas,	□	
Andres Flores,	AF	
Mary M. Thompson,	N	

DAWSON CO.—FORT CLARK P. O.

Name	Brand	Mark
W. E. Pafford,	WP	
E. M. Pafford,	TP	
Randolph Pafford,	♡	
Paulina Allen,	✝	

UVALDE P. O.

Name	Brand	Mark
Pleasant Wright,	PW	
Sam. Spears,	SS	
Samuel Cantwell,	℘	

BANDERA CO.—BANDERA P. O.

Name	Brand	Mark
Albert Adamietz	A (circled)	
James Bandy	A	
Thomas Bandy	JO	
O. B. Miles	M (circled)	
J. W. Phillips	∩	
J. D. Sauer	CI	*
do.	*S (circled)	
W. A. Lockart	A	
David Munroe	D	
James J. Bandy	A	
Miss. M. M. Chipman	T	

BANDERA COUNTY.

21

Name	Brand	Mark
George Hay,	HAY	
do.	Ⓗ	
Mrs. J. Hay,	JH	
B. F. Bird,	B	
do.	BIRD	
Miss Armenia Bird,	B[	
Charles Bird,	B	
Amasa Clark,	AC	
do.	AC	
E. A. Chipman,	EC	
Mrs. S. Gibson,	G2	
L. Haywood,	LH	

BANDERA COUNTY.

Name	Brand	Mark
A. Hoffman,	AH	⋈ ⋈
do.	HH	⋈ ⋈
do.	*AH	⋈ ⋈
J. W. Harrington,	OX	⋈ ⋈
A. Klappenbach,	AK	⊂⊃
John Kindla,	KT	⋈ ⋈
T. L. Miller,	71 ⋈	⋈ ⋈
Casper Kalka,	2	⋈ ⋈
Joseph Kalka,	JK	⋈ ⋈
Mrs. Elizabeth Laxon,	Ⓛ	⋈ ⋈ * ⋈
do.	*27	⋈ ⋈
Samuel C. Mott,	S	⊂⊃

BANDERA COUNTY.

Name	Brand	Mark
Thomas Miller,	M	
Mrs. Martha Miller,	O	
H. C. McKay,	HM	
do.	▢	
do.	*36	
Joseph Moravetz,	4O	
E. Oberski,		
do.	*	
Joseph Onion,	JE	
Joseph Poor,	P	
J. P. Rodriguez,	PR	

BANDERA COUNTY.

Daniel Rugh,	RU	
Joseph Sutherland,	M	
do.	J	
Thos. Hayduk,	W	
F. Juretzky,	F	
J. B. Miller,	O	
John A. Jones.	AJ	
do.	HS	
do.	IJ	
J. T. Stephens,	S	
Mary M. Rine,	ՈΛ	

MEDINA COUNTY.   25

Thomas Mazwreck,

Frank Waclawzyk,

do.

MEDINA CO. CASTROVILLE P. O.

G. H. Noonan,

do.

H. Benseman,

C. F. Goldberg,

J. Becker,

Joseph Bendele,

Andres Haby,

Ambrose Haby,	F	
Valentine Hass,	VH	
Peter Jungmann,	MP	
H. Zinsmister,	◇4	
do.	*Z4	
Peter Heineman,	A	
Catarena Wagner.	♈	
do.	ÆB	
Joseph Burrell,	₿	
Mrs. Barbra Taschler,	T	
do.	*T/⬠	

MEDINA COUNTY. 27

T. C G. Becker,	⊁B⊃	⊂⊃
Mathias Becker,	MB	⊂⊋
do.	J	⊂⊋
J. B. Wernett, jr.	TM⊖⊋.⊂⊃	
Louis Mehring,	AL ⊂⊋.⊂⊃	
Nicholas Hoffman,	'HO	⊂⊋
do.	·HM	⊂⊃
Julius Heuchling,	⌒/T	⊖⊃
Len Moore,	LON	⊖⊋
do.	LO	⊖⊋
Jacob Koenig,	JP	⊖⊋

MEDINA COUNTY.

Name	Mark			
Jacob Haby,	6O	⊂⊃	⊂⊃	⊂⊃
Miss. Mary Haldy,	8C			⊂⊃
H. T. Renken,	|||			⊂⊃
do.	|||			
	*F'			⊂⊃
C. V. Ketchum,	ZT			⊂⊃
Jacob Zimmerli,	INO			⊂⊃
do.	*Z8			⊂⊃
Miss. Lyda P. Boyls,	B			⊂⊃
Valentine Guly,	↳	⊂⊃	⊂⊃	
do.	*↳	⊂⊃	⊂⊃	
John Hoffmann,	Ǝ₁			⊂⊃

MEDINA COUNTY.

Anthon Schneider,	ĀS	
do.	AS	
John Lamon,	5L	
do.	JL	
do.	5L	
do.	5L	
do.	5L	
John Vance,	V̂	
do.	*y	
Francis Steinle,	⅁	
do.	◊	

MEDINA COUNTY

Name	Brand	Mark
Mrs. R. Jungman,	⊤	
Mrs. C. Jungman.	M	
Joseph Saltner,	S	
Nicholas Tschierhardt,	SS	
John G. Turpe,	GT	
do.	OH	
do.	H	
Joseph Maear,	57	
Joseph Conrad,	C J	
Johseph Kempf,		
Joseph Schorp,	SΔ	
Joseph Bader, sr.		

MEDINA COUNTY

Name	Brand	Mark
Sebastian Bader,	66	⊂⊃
Henry Haass,	⊤⃝	⊖⊃
Mss. Martha Haby,	H	⊂⊃
S. Boon,	SB	
J. R. Owings,	H	⊖⊖ *⊂⊃
Chas. de Montel,	⚓	⊖⊖
Mary Bader,	☆	⊂⊖
Joseph Bader,	☆	⊂⊖
Geo. Haass,	HC	⊂⊖
do.	*HG	⊖⊖
Mrs. A. M. Haass,	⅏	⊖⊃

Mrs. Mary Spattel,	S P	
August Weber,	33	
do.	R	
John Kohl,	22	
Joseph Notter.	⚒	*
Peter F. Pengenot	F	
Louis Huth,	H	
George Mangold sr.,	M	
George Mangold jr.,	M 7	*
John Deras,	JUI	
do.	5F	

MEDINA COUNTY. 33

W. C. Mullen,	SM
John Kreissle,	⌒L
James Lee,	⌒L
Mrs. Minerva Harr,	⌒
do·	82
John T. Lytle,	L
Michael Neagelin, jr.	NE
Joseph Weber,	⌓J
Jacob Koenig.	7K
Joseph Schneider,	105
do.	◎

3

MEDINA COUNTY.

Name	Brand	Marks
John Merian,		
Joseph Bilharz,	JB	
G. L. Haass,	H	
do.		
Roman Gross,	RG	
do.	VO	
do.	RC	
Nicholas Haby,	NS	
Joseph Krust,		
Miss. Jennie Krust	NA	
John Itk,	JJ	

MEDINA COUNTY.

Owner	Brand	Earmark
Michael Nagelin,	MN	
John Haberle,	O-O	
do.	JF	
Mrs. Catharine Deres,	MC	
Jos. Conraud,	♡	
do.	C3	
Seraphim Itis,	7	
Joseph Mann,	JM	
Richard Mechler,	ME	
do.	*ME	
do.	74	

Alois Walker,	AW	⚬⚬
Samuel Herfurth,	2H	⚬⚬
John Herfurth,	ⱻH	⚬⚬
Ferdinand Niggle,	JUL	⊖⊝
do.	*O	⚬⚬
Peter Chassard,	A⊣	⚬⊃
do.	*10	⚬⊃
George Christillis,	5B ⊖⊝ *	⚬⚬
do.	2C	⊖⊝
Mrs. M.S. Christillis	GC	⚬⚬
Joseph Christillis,	4	⊖⊝

Andres Bendela,	B+	
Fr Gutzeit,	117	
do.		
Leonhard Peteriet,	P.S	
Edward Brown,	WI	
Mrs. D. Brown,	WB	
do.	ONE	
Philip Haass,	PH	
Gerhard Ihnken,	5J	
do.		

MEDINA COUNTY.

Name	Brand	Earmark
Mrs. Teresa Grunewald,	FG	⊂⊃
James Paul,	FS	⊂⊃
Jacob Bendele,	B3	⊖⊖
Martin Schmedt,	□	⊖⊃
John Liesberg,	JL	⊂⊃
Frank Kappart,	ꝺ	⊖⊖
do.	☂	⊖⊖
Louis Haby,	HƎ	⊂⊅*⊂⊃
Z. Jung,	⟨A⟩	⊂З
Mrs. S. E. Ketchum,	CV	⊂⊖
Benhard Bock,	ΛZ	⊂Ƨ*⊂⊃

MEDINA COUNTY.

Fredrick Haass.	U	
do.	HF	
do.	Ⓑ	
Nicholas Tondre.	NT	
Eugene Tondre,	NT	
D. B. Moore,	DBM	
do.	*EM	
H. M. Moore,	L O	
S. T. Heath,	LH	
Louis Heath,	XCD	
Jessie Heath,	JES	

MEDINA COUNTY.

Valentine Vollmer,	V I	
Peter Conrad,	CP	
W. Tomlin,	U C On Hip,	
A. Tomlin,	U C On Side,	
do.	M	
do.	SJ	
John B. Burrell,	ℑ	
do.	H O	
A. Allen,	A 6	
August Mechler,	A	
do.	A 2	

MEDINA COUNTY. 41

James Blackaller,	UL	(brand)

NEW FOUNTAIN P. O.

Fredrick Haler,	2I	(brand)
Mrs. H White,	LW	(brand)
Ludwig Mumme,	LM	(brand)
Henry Hartman,	FP	(brand)
Daniel McLamore,	CM	(brand)
Memke M Saathoff,	⚯	(brand)
Henry Gerdis,	MG	(brand)
George Leinweber,	JL	(brand)
do.	*JL	(brand)
R. Stiegler,	110 (brands)	

MEDINA COUNTY

Name	Brand	Mark
John D. Shien,	ZU	
do.	DT	
S. A. Long,	☽	
do.	*SL	
do.	*SL	
Gottleab Steigler,	SG	
Paul Oefinger,	PL	
Adam Bless,	BL	
Wm. Schumacher,	W/L	
Christian Schumacher,	2E	
George Speyer,	5I	
Didrick Huschen,	BE	

MEDINA COUNTY

Andres Oefinger,	A O	⟩⟨
John Grosenbacher,	O	⟩⟨
August Leinweber,	C5	⟩◐* ⟩⟨
do.	L	⟩⟨
Albeg. Meyer,	[A]	◐◑* ⟩⟨
Julius Harstung,	ꝋ	◐●
W. A. Burrows.	Ω	⊃⊂
John B. Burrows,	JBB	⊃⊂
Gottf. Stiegler,	CS	⟩⟨
do.	╫	⟩⟨
Isaac H. King,	JK	⊕⊖

W. H. Harper,	O͡A	
John L. Harper,	J͡H	
do.	JH	
G. W. Harper,	OA	
do.	◇H◇	
do.	⊕H	
do.	A	
Ann L. Harper,	Æ	
Rorace P. King.	Æ	
George Redus,	SOT	
John Redus.	V2	
Tally Burnett,	UD	

MEDINA COUNTY.   45

John Nietenhofer,	5O	
do.	HE	
do.	*HE	
W. S. Hutchison,	H̃	
John Reitzer,	JR	
Ambrose Reitzer,	AR	
G. G. Vanpelt,	TE	
G. G. Vanpelt & Bros.,	TB	
do.	Y	
E. L. Dean,	ED	
John Leinweber,	UL	

MEDINA COUNTY.

Fredrick N. Oltmann,	ST	⌀	D.	⌀
do.	FN		⌀	
do.	D4		⌀	
Wilson Beckley,	TCU		⌀	
Gerd Gerdes,	G	⌀	⌀	
Jacob Riff,	JR		⌀	
E. Aden,	EA		⌀	
John Heyer,	JH		⌀	
Henry Pechler,	I-P		⌀	
Adolph Tampke,	AT	⌀	⌀	
W. G. McDonald,	T		⌀	

MEDINA COUNTY.

Name	Brand	Earmark
Mrs. E. Bailey,	MR	
do.	S D	
do.	S-D	
Harm Baizan,	Hb	
do	T	
Joseph Decker,	J	
Franciska Wantz,	IW	
R. Schoroling,	S	
do.	HH	
A. Eit.	A	
H. Borchers,	HB	

MEDINA COUNTY.

John H. Denis,	HD	CΞ
Foke Saathoof.	S1 CƆ * CƆ	
Mrs. Catrena Bender,	н	ΞƆ
Mrs. D. Rieden,	JZ	CƆ
do.	Q- JZ	CƆ
Remi Marques,	RM	CƆ
do	BK	ΞƆ
T. P. Malone,	PM	
Jacob Riff,	JR	CƆ
T. Otto Grell	JOG	CƆ

MEDINA COUNTY.

G. H. Faseler,	GF	
John H. Weimers,	HW	
A. J. Long,	AL	
W. H. Long,	TL	
John Sturm,	IST	
Louis Boehle,	LB	
do,	Q LB	
Wilson Bailey,	RR	
John Oefinger,	EQ	
Fredrick Roelf,	RF	

Name	Brand	Marks
Christian Eckhart,	ꓶE	
S. Schweers,	Sꓶ	
do.	ꓘ	
do.	ꓶF	
do.	ꓶF	
Albert Tampke,	ꓶ	
Andreas Martin,	MA	
Mrs. M. Smith,	LV	
do.	*LV	
T. J. Johnson,	JJ	
G. S. Johnson,	◇J◇	

Name	Brand	Mark
J. B. McLamore,	JBM	
Nicholas Winkler,	NW	
J. J. Simpson,	OB	
do	O̅B̅	
Gottlieb Britsch,	GB	
Adolph Nietenhofer,	JN	
O. N Oltmann,	N2	
A. N. Oltmann,	AN	
Henry Brooks,	hb	
William Redus,	◇ (with ∽ inside)	
Wm. Heien.	25	

MEDINA COUNTY.

Owner	Brand	Earmark
G. W. Robbins,	CR	
do.	RP	
John H. Gerdes.	IC (reversed)	⊃⊂
M. M. Saathoff,	MS (reversed)	⊂⊃
do.	*MS (reversed)	⊂⊃
Fred. Munnink,	FF (reversed)	⊃⊂ *⊂⊃
Harm Bohmfalk,	ST	⌒⌒
John Saathoff,	IS	⊂⊃
do.	BF	⊂⊃
Frank Schulte,	SF (reversed)	⊂⊃
H. H. Balzen,	BB (reversed)	⌒⌒

MEDINA COUNTY. 53

George Redus,	GR	
Mrs. L. Smith,	RST	
do.	SB	
do.	RS	
C. Eckhardt,	7E	
M. A. McCombs,	63	
M. Davis,	ND	
E. M. Downs,	⃞B	
do.	7	
do.	⊗	
C. Wiemer,	⋈	

DHANIS P. O.

Wm. Myrick,	⅄	C3
F. Mayer,	MF	
J. W. Miller,	RW	C3
do.	JM	C3
R. C. Miller,	ᴕT	CƆ
do.	RM	CƆ
G. W. Miller,	ᴕT	C3
Mrs. R. Wolf,	)C2	CƆ
Jacob Wolf,	∨	∞

MEDINA COUNTY.

Name	Brand	Mark
Wm. Smith,	I J I	
Robt. Dorn,	A	
do.	✳⊕	
W. M. Kelly,	Wk	
John Kelly,	JK	
N. L. Kelly,	ℳK	
Joseph Ney,	NE I	
Ney & Reily,	O	
A. H. Gohlson,	ℳ	
Henry Allof,	ⵗ	
A. Schuhmacher,	8	

MEDINA COUNTY.

Emory Gibbons,	E	
do.	2K	
do.	96	
H. Weynand,	WH	
M. H. Langford,	MS	
John Elam,	JE	
Jeff. Elam,	E	
John Johnson,	IJ	*
Peter Britz,	PB	
John Reinart,	J3	

MEDINA COUNTY.   57

Name	Brand	Earmark
John Reinhardt,	J 3 I	
Oliver Lee,	JTL	
Martin Bolt,	MB	
Mrs. M. Chambers,	M	
Oliver Jones,	OJ	
Mrs. S. T. Gibson,	G2	
John H. Cosgrove,	JC	
John Binnion.	NX	
do.	SO	
Wm. Porter,	WP	
P. G. Snow,	SNO	

Chas. Bolt,	B B	
do.	⌓	
do.	B	
Wm. Jones,	77	
Jacob Postert,	8P	
do.	WO	

KARNES CO.—Helena P. O.

Chas. A. Russell,	ꟼR	
G. W. Rhymes,	W	
Mrs. C. A. Rhymes,	CI	
Miss. Florence Davis,	ꟼD	

KARNES COUNTY.

D. G. Scogin.	F	
Mrs. Nancy Chesner,	JA	C3
A. Austin,	AU	C3
	*C3	C3
do.	*HT	C3
do.	*H	C3
do.	*P R	C3
do.	*HT	C3
do.	*CAE	C3
J. L. Smidt,	FS	
N. W. Eckford,	FIL	C3
do.	Z	

KARNES COUNTY.

W. R. Calloway.	S	
do.	C	
W. B. Reagan,	55	
do.	J	
do.	*UO	
L. C. Watkius,	LC	
do.	*7C	
D. C. Lyons,	DL	*
J. Sullivan,	10	
do.	SC	
do.	CO	
George Williams,	∩	

KARNES COUNTY.

Name	Brand	Ear marks
A. O. & J. Strickland,	Ⓢ	● ● ●
Mrs. A. Pullian,	XP	● ●* ●
J. F. Rhymes,	F̄	●
J. M. Little.	IXL	●
do.	7XI	
Joseph A. McCrabb,	J A	●
Isham Davis,	ID	
W. J. Rhymes,	HUK	●
do.	*UK	●
do.	*J C	●
Mrs. Nancy Parker,	JP	●
Daniel Hodges,	DH	●

Gordon Case,	◇	
L. S. Lawhon,	L	
John L. King,	JK	
do.	*JK	
H. J. Clark,	JR	
Thos. Chandler,	LC	
Hiram Silvers,	J	
Orin Drake,	OD	
do.	JL	
do.	P3	
Jonn M. Reagin,	MR	

James P. King,	◇		
do.	IV		
Tayler Crain,	U	On Shoulder,	
G. W. Crain,	U	Horses on thigh, Mares on hip.	
Thos. H. Puckettt,	⊢P		
do.	P		
A. B. Butter,	2B		
James B. Butter,	B		
J. R. Coke,	R		
J. H. Barfield,	X̂		
John D. Crain,	IF		

KARNES COUNTY.

Name	Brand	Mark
George Cooper,	+	(ear marks)
Morgon Coltrain,	9I	
J. B. Borroum,	7+	(ear marks)
do.	ⓉO	
V. F. Coke,	U4 On left hip,	
do.	⌀ On right hip,	(ear marks)
F. B. S. Coke,	UL	(ear marks)
A. R. Newman,	N	(ear marks)
J. W. Baylor,	◇	(ear marks)
John Weston,	⊍P	(ear marks)
R. F. Haskins,	2y	(ear marks)

KARNES COUNTY.

Name	Brand	Mark
W. H. Mayfield,	L	⊃⊂ ⊃⊂*
do.	7L	
do.	*L7	
E. A. Mayfield,	AM	⊂⊃
do.	65	
C. J. Barefield,	Ⓖ	⊂⊃
J. D. Cooper,	DC	⊂⊃•
Mrs. Martha Ricks,	RIX	⊃⊂
H. D. Ford,	HF	⊂⊃•
John Sumner,	56	⊃⊂
H. R. Ammons,	LA	⊂⊃

KARNES COUNTY.

Name	Brand	Mark
Mrs. M. E. Ratliff,	ZD	
Joseph Robertson,	IS	
Mrs. L. Williams,	L	
J. S. Carmichael,	FC	
John Sullivan,	SC	
Wm. Mitchell,	VE	
Mrs. Mary McCrabb,	M	
J. M. Jones,	J21	
Mrs. Sarah Flippin,	SM	
George W. Porter,	d	
T. C. Tomlinson,	TT	

KARNES COUNTY. 67

C. M. Tomlinson,	T3	
Burnel Butter,	BB	
J. M. Elder,	16	
John M. Yeary,	2Y	Horse Brand,
J. M. Reese,	JO	
do.	*JO	
John S. Wyche,	UT	
do.	*6	On thigh,
Charles Liles,	CL	
do.	CL	
T. J. C. Reese,	ↄ	

H. H. McLane,	JW		
do.	*J2		
do.	*JW		
do.	M	Horse Brand,	
do.	*TE		
W. J. McLane,	M	On Cattle only.	
do.	*TX		
do.	*▱		
do.	M̂	Horse Brand,	
S. Perryman,	SP		
J. A. McLane,	SF		

KARNES COUNTY.

Puckett & McLane,	TP	
L. D. Cook,	VL	
Cook & Wright,	V	
G. W. Brown,	S	
Mrs. Martha Yates,	3Y	
do.	V	
do.	SY	
do.	UY	
F. B. S. Cocke,	F	
Wanzer & Teller,	UF	
N. B. Evans,	3	

KARNES COUNTY.

Name	Brand	Marks
J. A. Wishert,	JH	(marks)
do	S3	(marks)
do.	⊥I	
A. W. Talk,	Ā	(marks)
J. E. Darden,	7L	(marks)
do.	⊥⊤	(marks)
W. G. Roark,	Һ	(marks)
John Littleton,	⌒U	(marks)
J. D. Newberry,	S̄	(marks)
L. D. Puckett,	ID	(marks)
do.	EK	

KARNES COUNTY.

Thos. Rabb,	TI	
do.	T8	
do.	TE	
J. C. Barfield,	JJJ	
do.	¢	
J. W. Campbell,	℞	
R. Ratliff,	+B	
do.	55	
Noel Bowen,	NB	
do.	⊢5	
P. H. Rose,	V	

KARNES COUNTY.

Mrs. R. Newman,	RN	
Mrs. R. Archie,	A	
L. S. Lipscomb,	LIP	
do.	JJ	
J. J. Ratliff,	23	
F. C. Wilburn,	FW	
do.	W	
John Talk,	P	
※		
Mrs. Sarah Little,	LL	
Mrs. S. M. Lawhon,	WL	

KARNES COUNTY. 73

PANAMARIA P. O.

Mathews Urbanzik,	(house symbol)	⊂⊃
John Rzeppa,	(key symbol)	⊙⊙
Anton Opiela,	Č	⊂⊃
Frank Biela,	(symbol)	⊂⊃
Caspar Brondar,	CB	⊂⊃
J. L. Short,	21	
Bishop & Johnson,	D5	E⊃
do.	IU	E⊃
H. M. Beverly,	50	⊂⊃
Lucas Moy,	LM	E⊃

KARNES COUNTY.

F. Kalus,	ꟻ2	⊂⊃
Albert Czerner,	I P	⟨⊃⟨⊃
Paul Banduch,	B	⊖⊖
John Kuhnel,	C K	⊂•⊃⊂⊃•
do.	C̽K̽	
Adam Labus,	V I	
Anna Opiela,	P	⊂⊃
Michael Brysh,	I X	⊖⊃
Frank Yozko,	Oi On Shoulder.	⊂⊃•
Mary Yozko,	Oi On Hip,	
do,	⌒12	

KARNES COUNTY. 75

Joseph Piegza,	Zi
John Rabstein,	JR
Dominik Keller,	ZK
John Dziuk,	JD
Albert Dugi,	DU
Simon Bronder.	BR
J. R. Skiles	JRS
Miss. Mary D. Skiles,	JRS
H. B. McLean,	JRS
Frank Kotzur,	F
Lorenz Szebanik,	4F

KARNES COUNTY.

Name	Brand	Mark
G. M. Collingsworth,	HK	
do.	88	
do.	⊤⋂⋂	
J. A. Tivy,	A̅	
do.	V̲	
J. L. Calvert,	JT	
do.	CA	
do.	HC	
Frank Kroll,	ƎK	
Joseph Sziegol,	⊕	
John Rosser,	℘V	
Trinidad Coy,	⋈	

KARNES COUNTY.

Name	Brand	Mark
Stephan Dietzman,	TX	
Frank Licy,	J6	
Jose Sanches.	LP	
B. F. Rosser,	UF	
Mrs. T. Coy,	℈T	
Jakob Opiela,	KO	
Nikolaus Opiela,	A	
John Opiela,	P	
Jakob Dworatzek,	⌂	
Joseph Caspick.	yO	
Frank Minka,	⋈A	

KARNES COUNTY.

Name	Brand	Mark
John Stirtz,	ⱶ	
Thos. Morzygemba,	◇–◇	
John Morzygemba,	△	
Filip Zerner,	FJ	
Albert Kniesky,	AK	
do.	FK	
Dominik Kolenda,	IE	
Joseph Morzygemba,	△	
Frank Burda,	FB	
Lorenz Wiatrik,	⁓Y	
Mrs. Marie Olynik,	FO	

Gervas Gabrisch,	SE	୧୨
Mrs. Mary Morzygemba,	M	CD
Joseph Kiriss,	KY	⊃⊂
Anton Bonk,	A	
Albert Kaspzik,	HK	୧୨
Lorenz Pawelick,	⚓	ED
John Gawlick,	ΩI	C⊃
John Kowoliek,	JK	⊃⊂
Michael Yoskula,	MJ	EƆ
Wm. F. Shott,	♂	CD
James Boone,	ꙮ	EƎ

KARNES COUNTY.

ECLETO P. O.

Wm. Hutchison,	SA	⊕⊃
R. A. Kelly,	OS	
Harvy Stanard,	WH	⊂⊃
do.	ՊՊ	
do.	I C I	⊂⊃
do.	W K	⊕⊃
Mrs. T. Dromgoole,	Ⓒ	⊕⊃
do.	WD	⊕⊃
W. H. Cochran,	◇C◇	
W. G. Belding,	B̂	⊃⊂

KARNES COUNTY.   81

B. Ford,	100
Colin Campbell,	F
do.	66
W. G. Kelly,	DE
do.	HK
M. A. Tyler,	*On Hip,* MT
do.	*On Shoulder* MT
do.	*On Side* MT
do.	*On Hip* MT (inverted)
do.	TAT

6

W. O. Hutchison,	IOI	
Solomon Brown.	H5	C⊃
J. B. Dees,	∩G	C⊃
do.	ђ	
W. S. Wilkinson,	WƎ	ƎϽ
do.	*EΛ	ӘϽ
	ƎϽ	C⊃
John Osmon,	SIM ӘϽ *C⊃	

YORKTOWN P. O.

J. A. Newman jr.,	☿	ϽϽ
Wm. Burt,	β	ϾϿ

WILSON COUNTY.

James Asher.	⊔A	(ear marks)
do.	⌐	
Florence Mahoney,	C	
Lockwood Birdsall,	AP	
do.	CC	

WILSON CO. Sutherland Springs P. O.

David T. Wheeler,	OW	(ear marks)
do.	7	(ear marks)
Wm. R. Goode,	UH	(ear marks)
J. E. Wheeler,	←W	(ear marks)
Jas. S. Morris,	∩∩	

WILSON COUNTY.

Name	Mark	
G. F. Harper,		
J. C. Butler,		
Louis Vollrath,		
Melcor Trabiaso,		
Manuel Trabiaso,		
Miguel Tores.		
Jose Marea Percs,		
Ysidro Orosco,		
Francisco Jimines,		
Euseris del Valle,		
Mrs. T. F. Seguin,		

WILSON COUNTY

Name	Brand	Mark
T. J. Peacock,	TP	
W. K. Baylor,	KB	
E. Potts,	EP	
C. M. Barclay,	U2	
do.	B	
E. S. Harper,	CH	
Jose Antonio Peres,	JA	
G. H. McDaniel,	US (reversed)	
R. B. Gilbert,	SG (reversed S)	
E. Nier,	3K	
John R. King,	K	

WILSON COUNTY.

Name	Brand	Mark
C. Rutherford,	7C	
J. J. Kilgore,	JK	⊂⊃
H. A. Gouger,	FS	⊂⊃
Charles Harper,	T (When on horses invariably upon thigh)	⊂⊃
Nicolas de los Santos,	⅄	⊂⊃
do.	NS	
Bernardino Ruiz,	Ꙭ	⊂⊃
Vecinte Cantu,	VC	⊂⊃
Juan Cantu,	CAT	⊂⊃
C. Martines,	UF	⊂⊃
Ramon de la Zarda,	RƖ	⊂⊃

WILSON COUNTY.

Nemecio de la Zerda,	N̯	
T. Castaneda,		
Bartolo Ortiz		
Miss. Librado Flores,	LF	
Frailan de la Garza,		
G. Arciuega,	A	
Jesus Peres,	JP	
Josefa Valdez,	JV	
B. Goodwin,	ne	
do.	BEN	

WILSON COUNTY.

G. W. Hitchings,	77	
do.	㇀	
do.	⟂ (with *)	
do.	RK (with *)	
do.	CƆ	
Nepumnseuo Aguilar,	☆R	
Mrs. G. F. Seguin,	G	
Cesario Carmona,	⩘	
L. Trivino,	ᒪo	
Ma. de Jesus P. de la Zerda,	Å	
Pilar Trivino,	Ⅎ	

WILSON COUNTY.

Name	Brand	Mark
Jose M. Yvaneo,	ҶS	
Juan F. Flores,	ӔF	
W. D. Scull,	TA	
do.	*TA	
do.	*AD	
G. J. Houston,	GJH	
Russel Houston,	UN	
Mrs. E. Wayman,	W	
G. J. & R. Houston,	ZZ	
do.	On Side ℏ On Hip Ƴ	
C. Rector,	HM	

WILSON COUNTY.

Name	Brand	Mark
James Barnes,	JP	
J. McDaniel,	JD	
Melchor Jimenes,		
N. Flores,	NF	
Antonita Peres,	AP	
M. Hernandez,		
Mrs. M. L. S. de Flores,	LS	
do.	JMF	
A. G. Pickit,	P8	
do.	NP	
Agapeto Cantu,	A	

WILSON COUNTY.

S. W. Barker,	⟊	
Jose M. Roxo,	MR	
do.	H	
Mrs. C. F. de Zaragoza,	F	
do.	L	
Juan Peres,	P	

GRAYTOWN P. O.

M. C. Herrera,	HF	
do.	R	
do.	H	
Macedonia Mirando,	CL	

WILSON COUNTY.

Name	Brand	Ear Mark
Yssidro Flores,	I2F	
Mrs. Juana Castillo,	NC	
Henry Holdusen,	NR	
Beneto Cruz,	BI	
Jose A. Ruiz,	AR	
do.	E	
Rafala Herrera,	H	
Juan Delgado,		
Refugio Delgado,		
J. N. Rodriguez,	NR	
do.	On Jaw Z	

WILSON COUNTY.

Name	Brand	Marks
Matias Curvier,		
Casemiro Garza		
do.	03	
Juan Bueno,		
Ysabel Anya,		
Antonio Duian,		
Francisco da la Garza,		
Jesus Aldrete,		
Juan Talamantes,		
Pedro Flores,		
Esteven Pantoga,		

WILSON COUNTY.

Name	Brand	Mark
Nicolas Cruz,		
Jose M. Avala,		
do.		
Jose Flores,		
Antonio Jimenes,		
Mrs. T. Montoya,		
do.		
Jose M. Menchaca,		
Simon Talamantes,		
Cline & Holduson,		
Henriques Garsa,		

WILSON COUNTY.

Name	Brand	Mark
Hilario Montoyo		
do.		
Jose M. Delgado,		
Filipe Samora,		
Pabla Sauseda,		
Dario Talamantes,		
Miguel Gil,		
Barnabe Menchaca.		
do.		
Beanino Falcau,		

WILSON COUNTY.

Name	Brand	Mark
Juan Jimenes,		
Juan Bala,		
Francisco Estrada,		
Dimas Gonzales,	GL	
Florintina Lopes,		
Ygnacio Gil,		
do.		
Juan Curvier,		
Narcissa Prue,	AP	
Antonio Gonzales,		

WILSON COUNTY.

Name	Brand	Mark
Manuel Zepeda,	MF	
do.	NA	
Miguel Yndo,	R	
Pedro Reyes.	PR	
Decidora Sanchez,	S	
Cresencio Hernandez,	元	
Jose Zepeda,	⅄	

LAVERNIA P. O.

Name	Brand	Mark
James Summerville,	S	
H. Yelvington,	HY	
R. B. Hudson,	JR	

BEE COUNTY.

RANCHO P. O.

Cone, Walker & Co.,	CONE	⊃⊂
do.	AC	On left Shoulder,

BEE CO. BEEVILLE P. O.

Miss. H. Sullivan,	HP	⊃⊂
Ira Mullin or Agt.,	IW	⊂⊃
Thos. J. Smith,	JS	⊂⊃
S. F. Wright,	W	⊃⊂
W. R. Hayes,	⌒	⊃⊂ * ⊂⊃
John Hynes,	JH	⊂⊃

BEE COUNTY. 99

J. B. New,	NU	
Mrs. M. Williamson,	MW	
J. Turner or Agt.,	JL	
Mrs. Cleopatria Rupe,	R	
E. T. Fuller,	F	
Ed. Sedgwick.	S O	
Mrs. J. Mullin or Agt.	M2	
J. P. Wilson,	FS	
John A. Nutt,	U	

D. C. Grover,	C ℔ ⊖⊝*⊖⊝	
J. A. Bignar,	ℬ	⊖⊝
D. W. Suliivan,	ⅅ	⊖⊝
R. E. Nutt,	NU	⊂⊃
do.	U	
Mrs. J. E. Dodd,	DOD	⊂⊃
Thos Lynch,	ℸL	⊂⊃
Mrs. D. Robeson,	⊒D	⊖⊝
do.	⊝D	⊖⊝
do.	⊀D	⊖⊝
John Fadden,	F⏋	⊂⊃

BEE COUNTY. 101

Owner	Brand	Ear mark
D. A. T. Walton,	T2	
do.	INOU	
do.	ONO	
W. B. Roberts,	LR	(ear mark)
do.	J	(ear mark)
Jas. & J. E. Wilson,	J On Side.	(ear mark)
J. E. & J. P. Wilson,	J On Hip.	(ear mark)
J. E. Wilson,	Ꮈ	(ear mark)
S. P. H. Williams,	PH	(ear mark)
do.	27	(ear mark)
Geo. W. Grover or Agt.,	K	(ear mark)

BEE COUNTY.

B. O. Williams or Agt.,	A	⊃⊂
do.	AB	⊂⊃
B. M. G. Allsup or Agt.,	JE	⊃⊂
do,	E	⊃⊂
Mrs. P. Whitby or Agt.,	4 7	⊂⊃
do.	G	⊂⊃
T. M. & R. A. Allsup,	TA	⊂⊃
do.	S	
Mrs. N. C. Allsup,	S⁻	
J. W Park or Agt,	JP	⊃⊂
Wm. Park or Agt,	♂	⊂⊃

Wm. Miller,	RM	
do.	TR	
do.	(T over diamond)	
do,	(T over diamond)	
N. C. Webster,	(diamond over T)	
do.	♂	
Ephram H Spalding,	O / I	
David A. Webster,	A / I	
T. B. Zumwalt or Agt.,	TZ	

BEE COUNTY.

David R. May,	JK	Ǝ3
do.	MAY	
T. Fuller Estate of,	Ⓐ	
J. P. Ryan,	JR	⊙⊃
Hugh Parsons,	HP	
do.	*J	
Vincent Holt,	VH	
P. B. Irvin,	72	⊂⊙
Mrs. W. Fisher,	27	
James Brown,	Bl	⊃⊂
J. H. Fox,	JH	⊂⊙

BEE COUNTY.

J. S. Wright,	SW	⊖• ⊖
do.	W̄	⊖• ⊖
Howell, Flint & Tumlinson,	F	
Eugene Grover,	NC	⊖ ⊖ * ⊇ ⊃
A. Fitzgerald or Agt.,	F9	⊇ ⊃
do.	7S	⊂• ⊃
Wm. Hynes,	VH	⊂ ⊃•
do.	*EB	⊂ ⊃•
J. A. Phelps,	JAP	⊖• ⊃
Miss. M. J. Bradley & Sisters,	5B	⊂•• ⊃
Giles Carter,	69	⊂•• ⊃•

BEE COUNTY.

John Atkins,	5A	⊖⊃*⊂⊖
Mrs. P. Scott,	NS	⊖⊇
do.	ꓴ	
T. S. Tyson,	C+	⊂●⊃*⊂⊃
do.	T̂	⊂●⊃
do.	*JCT	⊂⊃
do.	▽T	⊂⊃
F. J. Mullin or Agt.,	FM	⊖●
A. W. Thresher,	UK	⊂⊇
J. M. Foster,	JF	⊂⊐
J. M. McCollom,	Â	⊖●

Mrs. Ellen Corrigan,	J C	⊂⊃ *⊕⊇
do.	*P P	⊂⊃
do.	*F A	⊂⊃
J. P. Dykes,	L D	⊂⊃
do.	S B	⊂⊃
Patrick Burk,	B U	⊂⊃
do.	◇P	⊂⊃
Michae Carroll,	N 3	⊂⊃
Wm. Carroll,	B U	⊂⊃
John Carroll,	U B	⊂⊃
Wm. Jones,	A̶J	⊂⊙

BEE COUNTY.

W. A. Kennedy,	ƍ-	⊖⊖
R. E. Winn Est. of,	RW	⊖●
Mrs. M. Young,	H	
Mrs. D. D. Odom,	A	⊖⊖
C. C. Jones,	7J	⊖⊖
do.	Ǝ	⊖⊖
do.	⊙	
M. Seligson,	△S	⊖⊖
J. H. Althouse,	၇	⊂⊖
Mrs. E. L. Parker,	⊥	⊂⊖ *⊂⊖
M. G. Fellers,	NF	

BEE COUNTY.

R. M. Robeson,	R̂	⊖⊃
Henderson Williams,	⊬E	⋈
do.	⊬E	⋈
do.	L A	⋈
do.	JHS	⋈
do.	⊬E	⋈
do.	EP	⋈
do.	ŷ	⋈
do.	⊣E	⋈
W. M. Parchman,	W	⊖⊃
J. B. Maddry,	JH	⋈
James Wilson.	W	⊖⊃

BEE COUNTY.

M. Fox Est. of	MF	CD
do.	F (crossed)	
J. C. Steen.	44	E∃
do.	Ⓐ	CD
Mrs. E. E Mitchell,	ϾC	E∃
Archibald Martin,	∀	⊗⊃
do.	ΛAT	CD
J. T. Hayden,	JH	⊃C
do.	JH	∃⊂
do.	HH	E∃
S. H. Smith,	S♡	E∃

110

BEE COUNTY.   111

H. T. Clare,	HC	
John I. Clare,	JIC	
J. F. Clare Est. of,	FC	
John McIver,	(brand)	
do.	*d	
do.	*JI	
Willis Parker,	P	
do.	m	
do.	JP	
C. L. Lockhart,	CW	
do.	W	

G. W. McClanahan,	JMC	
do.	JMC	
J. N. Lee,	HL	
do.	4	
H. R. May,	HM	
A. C. Jones or Agt.,	J	
Mrs. M. P. Thresher,	⅊	
F. P. Rawlings,	♡	
do.	*♡	
Miss. M. L. Rawlings,	♡	
Miss. E. B. Rawlings,	♡	

BEE COUNTY

Name	Brand	Mark
Miss. S. V. Rawlings,	♡	
Mrs. S. J. Robertson,	♡	
Jas. B. Rawlings	♡	
do.	WR	
H. A. Rawlings,	♡	
H. C. Ryan,	JE	
do.	*W̄	
do.	*J9	
Mrs. L. Ryan or Agt.,	8P	
John Weed,	⊔⊔⊔	
do.	SL	

BEE COUNTY.

Name	Brand	Mark
Alfred Weed,	P	(right & left crop)
do.	Ψc	(right & left crop)
do.	✝c	(right & left crop)
W. A. Scott,	AK	(right & left crop)
Thos. P. Scott,	8	(right & left crop)
Miss. Susan Scott,	8 8	(right & left crop)
C. B. Palmer,	CP	(right & left crop)
do.	JH	(right & left crop)
Mrs. C. Fuller ar Agt.,	CF	(right & left crop)
Mrs. S. Phelps,	ᛞ	(right & left crop)
do.	ᛈ	(right & left crop)

BEE COUNTY. 115

Benj. Barber,	2h	
do.	7)	
do.	Ỵ	
do.	3 2	
do.	3L	
Mrs. S. Campbell,	LC	
do.	SG	
do.	SG	
do.	22	
J. W. Robeson,	ER	
Wm. Leahy,	W	
Patrick Fadden,	PF	

BEE COUNTY.

G. B. McCollom,	C̅M̅	
do.	CM	
J. E. Little,	ꂅ	
do. *	Y	
do. *	O2	
Andrew Fox,	A̅F̅	
James Ryan,	J̅R̅	
do. *	JR	
Henry Ryan,	HR	
do.	*HR	
Chas. Bradley,	cB	
T. H. Marsden,	ꝑ	

ATASCOSA COUNTY. 117

RUFUGIO P. O.

J. Perkins,		
Jessie Perkins,		
Cader Perkins,		
Joshua Perkins,		
Jas. M. Tullos,		

ATASCOSA CO. Pleasanton P. O.

H. C. Fountain.		
do.		
J. O. C. Barksdale,		
W. J. Barksdale,		

Name	Brand	Mark
E. O'Bryan,	B over O	
L. Barksdale Est of,	EC	
Mrs. M. Barksdale or Agt,	K	
James Jolley,	J	
Miss. N. J. Jolley,	OMA	
L. B. Harrison,	S	
A. G. Martin,	AM	
Mrs. Mary Martin,	W	
Henry G. Martin,	#	
Miss. Mary Kotula,	J	
Mrs. Sophia Saltsman or Agt.,	S	

Name	Brand	Mark
Frank Saltsman,	R	
Frank Williams,	H	
L. D. Williams.	JT	
do.	T	
Louis Areola,	A	
Daniel Arnold,	DA	
Simpson McCoy.	T5	
do.	7H	
Miss. Francis Hill,	(swastika-like)	
Joseph Kotula,	F	
do.	*F	

ATASCOSA COUNTY.

Name	Brand	Earmark
L. W. Pierce.	HP	⊂⊃ ⊂⊃ * ⊂⊃
Miss. M. C. Dossey,	ƐD	⊂⊃
G. W. Dossey,	3D	⊂⊃
do.	P	⊂⊃
do.	Đ	
W. G. Dossey,	3D	⊂⊃
J. W. McMains,	ⱧN	⊂⊃
Urill Jones,	LT	⊂⊃
B. F. Fuller,	ROS	⊂⊃ * ⊂⊃
do.	*♢	⊂⊃
James H. Fuller,	F	⊂⊃
Aurices Esparsa,	ƐA	⊂⊃

ATASCOSA COUNTY.

T. A. Long,	T̄L	
do.	ĪD	
do.	ID	
Joel M. Walker,	JJ	
Mrs. Emily Walker,	22	
Jacob Ryman,	⬡	
F. Hall & Bro.,	HO	
do.	*T̄	
do.	*RH	*
do.	*8	On Side,
J. W. Bell,	W	

ATASCOSA COUNTY.

M. D. Bell,	T	⊃⊂
J. Antonio Navar.o,	A⁰	⊂⊃
S. S. Robinson or Agt.,	JL	⊂⊃
F. M. Mansfield,	J	⊂⊃
C. Y. Long,	ƆL	⊂⊃
do.	4 L	⊃⊂
do.	3L	⊂⊃
do.	HD	⊂Ƹ
Wm. Rogers or Agt.,	WR	⊃⊣
Mrs. A. Notgrass,	AR	⊂⊃
Simon Rodriguez,	ƧR	⊃⊂

ATASCOSA COUNTY.

Name	Brand	Mark
Senon Rodriguez,	SR	
Jesse L. Long,	JL	
Andrew McMains,	H	
Juan M. Tarin,	H	
Ygnacio Sotelo sen.,	IS	
Ygnacio Sotelo jr.,	YS	
J. D. Neal.	3	
J. P. Neal,	HP	
Refugio Areola,	RA	
Manuel Esparsa,	₱	

ATASCOSA COUNTY.

Name	Brand	Mark
Manuel Rodriguez,	MP	
Mrs. Guadeloupe Areola,	JA	
Juan Palasio,	F	
Isaac Carver,	HP	
Janario Palasio,	GP	
Wesley Tollett,	5	
do.	3	
Simon Rieder,	SR	
Miss. Caroline Aikmaun,	CE	
Miss. Rosina Fest,	F	
T. R. Foster,	RF	

ATASCOSA COUNTY.

Name	Brand	Mark
John Henshaw,	S P	
do.	♂	
Antonio Saucero,	⊥⊤	
N. P. Barksdale,	⟡	
L. F. Barksdale,	FR	
James C. Harrison,	JH	
Andrew J. Blevins,	CB	
Wm. N. Nichols.	A	
John Camp,	CAP	
do.	⅄	
do.	P	

ATASCOSA COUNTY.

Jacob West,	⌶L	⊖⊖
Mrs. Jane West,	5	⊖⊖
James West,	JA	⊖⊖
Wm. Kelly,	WK	⊖⊖
Irvin Jones,	IJ	⊂⊃
R. Hilburn,	RH	⊖⊖
do.	*RH	⊖⊖
Marcellus French,	JF	⊂⊃
do.	JF	⊂⊃
Bennet Musgrave,	⌒A	⊖⊖
Calvin Musgrave,	JF	⊂⊃ *⊖⊖

ATASCOSA COUNTY.

Name	Brand	Mark
Antonio Wieglendoz,	M̶ (with cross)	
do.	* W M	
do.	* A W	
C. Terry,	T	
Nathaniel Terry,	T (with X below)	
Juan Tarin,	J T	
M. Ribas,	JJ	
Antonio Tarin,	A⋇	
John Sherman,	JON	
do.	* S X	
do.	* C Λ	

ATASCOSA COUNTY.

Name	Brand	Mark
W. N. Gates,	∞	
Thos. Brite Est of,	COW	
do.	18	Horse brand on shoulder.
E. Fields,	∃2	
M. C. Beall,	P•	
Saml. H. Neill,	25	
do.	.7C	
B. F. Neill,	3B	
do.	A/	
Mrs. C. Winn,	CW	
Ed. Walker or Agt.	SW	

ATASCOSA COUNTY.

J. Q. Musgrave,	H̄	
Mrs. H. Tumlinson,	HT	
Miss S. J Tumlinson,	AE	
J. M. W. Tumlinson,	JJ	
J. W. Tumlinson,	JIM	
P. F. Tumlinson,	PT	
do. on shoulder	*♡	
Joseph Tumlinson,	Ā	
do.	*WT	
do	*J	

John S. Fuller,	Ꝑ	⊰⊱
do.	18 on thigh	
Mrs. M. J. Russell,	ꝗ ◇	⊰•⊱•
Chas. S. Russell,	⌐	⊙⊱
A. L. Oden,	A	⊂⊃
M. D. Oden,	d7	⊂⊃*⊂⊣
T. S. Oden,	TIM	⊂⊙
Mrs. Caroline Oden,	O	⊂⊃
G. D Gilliland,	♥	⊰⊃
do.	♡	
James West.	JA	⊂⊙⊃*⊣⊣

ATASCOSA COUNTY.

Rayborn Goin,	33	
do.	*33	
Mrs. M. J. Stevens,	HB	
do	*HB	
J. M. Harrison,	HE	
do.	HE	
C. S. Turner	OO	
do.	*8 On hip.	
Carr & Johnson,	CAR	
do.	*T	

Thos. E. Dickens,	ћ	
L. B. Harris,	H2	
do.	*⊕	
do.	*SF	
do.	*KH	
do.	*TJ∧	
do.	*SP	
do.	*H̄2̄ do	
L. H. Tournat,	⊢T	
do.	*Aω	
T. H. Props,	ⵑ	

ATASCOSA COUNTY.

Name	Brand	Mark
L. T. Ward,	T	
A. Allen,	A6	
John E. Evans,	EE	
G. W. West,	W2	
J. West,	3E	
David West,	D6	
Bud West,	B3	
W. & Martin Parchman,	WP	
do,	FP	
Lemuel Parchman,	LAP	
John Hill,	HIL	

ATASCOSA COUNTY

J. R. Smith,	72	⊖⊃⊖⊃
do.	*72	⊖⊃⊖⊃
Mrs. S. A. Cavender,	IC	⊙⊃⊙
do.	IE	⊙⊃⊙
do.	⌐	⊖⊃⊙
J. F. Cavender,	FC	⊖⊃
Robt. E. Neill,	30	⊙⊃⊃⊖⊃
do.	*N	⊖⊃
Joseph Williams,	2	⊂⊃
do.	⊳→	⊂⊃
Miss F. E. Cavender.	LEF	⊖⊃

ATASCOSA COUNSY.

Name	Brand	Mark
J. N. Kennard,	JN	
N. G. Kennard,	N3	
Mrs. Eliza Oden,	W	
H. J. Props,	HP	
Mrs. M. Frame or Agt.	MF	
Wm. Frame Est. of	WF	
John Brite,	JB	
James T. Peacock,	PP	
M. C. Yates,	MY	
Yates & Mansfield,	J on hip	
Wm. Morris sr.	M	

ATASCOSA COUNTY.

Name	Brand	Earmark
Wm. Morris jr.	M̊	
R. A. Curry,	3D	
John Dossey,	D̄	
H. Rodriguez,	HR	
Spencer Morris,	S T	
Louisa Martin.	£	
James A. Crawford,	◇	
Nathaniel Hay,	N	
Mrs. S. Skwortz,	Ⓢ	
do.	*Aw	
do.	*ⓦ	

ATASCOSA COUNTY.

W. Marshall,	EM	
do.	MT	
do.	S7	
do.	d5	
Antonio Paddea,	P̄	
do.	*P	
James Dial, jr.	d2	
do.	*DIA	
do.	*H5	
Wright Williams,	3	

138 ATASCOSA COUNTY.

Mrs. Eliza Hay,	7663*63	
Wm. F. Martin,	4E	
John Martin,	46	
Wm. Owens,	W S	
Mrs. C. Yow,	CY	
Mrs. C. Ridgway	J2	

SAN ANTONIO P. O.

G. W. M. Duck,	QK	
do.	*F	
Wm. Caruthers,	BC	

ATASCOSA COUNTY.

Mrs. A. Klempka,	VK		
J. W. & I. N. Cooper,	⊂|D	On Lip.	
do.	S|		
I. M. Cowan,	C̲		
do.	*⊂|D	on side	
S. H. White,	∪		
Juan Jose de la Cruz sr.	⊃		
Juan de la Cruz,	N°G		
Casper de la Cruz,	C PC		

ATASCOSA COUNTY.

Name	Brand	Mark
Fred Opperman,	ℜ	
Rafaela de la Cruz,	RC	
Lauro de la Cruz,	₤	
Levi Lewis,	I T	
Mrs. Mary Williams,	R Y	
Joseph Hoffman,	HM	
Aaron Ranbie,	V I	
W. McD. Stephens,	HM	
do.	*Ⓦ	

FRIO COUNTY

FRIO CO. CASTROVILLE P. O.

J. G. Woodward,	SUF	
do.	*ƆC	
M. Woodward,	SUF	
do.	*C On cattle.	
C. Woodward,	CAV	
do.	*SUF	
do.	*2V	
do.	*(H)	
do.	*C	
do.	C On horses.	

FRIO COUNTY.

PLEASANTON P. O.

Name	Brand	Mark
H. Bennett,	CO	⊖⊖
A. C. Bennett,	7B	⊖⊖
Mrs. M. Bennett,	HL	⊖⊖
Cicil Bennett,	2	⊖⊖
Daniel Bennett,	1O1	⊖⊖
do.	*□	⊖⊖
Mrs. M. English,	7E	⊖⊖
Jonathan English,	EL	⊖⊖
Mrs. Margaret English,	E	⊖⊖
Ed Burleson,	EBƆE*ƆƆ	

FRIO COUNTY. 143

Name	Brand	Mark
Henry Burleson,	HB	
Jacob & H. Burleson,	B	
H. M. Dougherty,	HD	
do.	*CR On shoulder	
do.	LE On left side	
do.	LE On right side	
Leonard Eastwood,	LE on right hip	
James Eastwood,	E	
Joseph Gardner,	G	
A. F. Gardner,	AFG	
J. E. Gardner,	JE	

FRIO COUNTY

B. F. Franks Est. of	☡	
J. B. Franks,	JF	
J. S. Mangum,	O	
do.	*⚹K	
W. Z. Mangum,	617	
G. M. Mangum	716	
N. T. Mangum	616	
Mrs. Caroline Berry	♡ on hip	
do	♡ on shoulder	
Miss M Berry	♡ on side	
Miss Ann E Berry	♡ On side.	

FRIO COUNTY.

Name	Brand	Mark
John Berry,	J♡	
do.	*♡	
J. B. Spears,	T6	
do.	ND	
Mrs. D. W. Williams,	JU	
Julius McKinney.	IC2	
do.	*J2	
Silas Hay,	S6	

DIMMIT CO. Eagle Pass P. O.

John Burleson,	RB	
do.	*LV	
do.	*EV	
do.	*JV	
do.	*D	
do.	2	
Wm. Dickins.	4	
do.	*EC	
Leonard L. Bell,	B	

COMAL CO. New Braunfels P. O.

J. J. Groos,	G	
Walther H. Preston,	P↓	
do.	ᎮᏢ	
Theo. Koester,	TK	
Jacob Brecher,	JB	
Friedrich Forster,	HF	
Daniel Stahl,	AS	
Julius Stahl,	42	
F. W. Reinarz,	WR	

148 COMAL COUNTY.

Name	Brand	Mark
John F. Torrey,	FT	
Samuel Mather,	(compass/A)	⊖⊖
do.	SM	
John Walzem,	Y	⊖⊖
A. J. Schneider,	↳	⊂⊃
Johann Schneider,	S3	⊂⊃
Conrad Meyer,	♊	⊂⊃
Carl Koch,	CK	⊂⊃
F. H. Faigaux,	ƆE	∞
do.	*E	∞

COMAL COUNTY. 149

Name	Brand	Mark
Herman Spiess,	SW	
Andres Pape,	AP	
F. J. Lindheimer.	⛢	⊳⊲ *
Felix Bracht,	ß	
Jacob Schmitz,	JJ	
Conrad Pape, sr.	OP	
Frances Grohs,	FG	
do.	IGI	
Charles Fischer,	F6	

COMAL COUNTY.

Name	Brand	Mark
Daniel Wiseman,	DW	⊂⊃
August Wolfshohl,	⅄⅄	⊖⊃
do.	*⊠	⊂⊃
John Trebes,	ƐT	⊂⊐
Martin Engelmann,	3̄ 6̄	⊙⊃
do.	*36	⊙⊃
John Katterle,	J A	⊂⊐
Mrs. Malinda B. Owen,	MT	⊞⊐
Mrs. Catharine Wengeroth,	CW	⊂⊃
Peter Trusch,	PT ⊂⊙⊃ *⊂⊃	
Jacob Herring,	△	⊟⊃

Otto Schmuck,	OSK	
John Wyel,	W2	
H. Rienninger,	HR	
Geo. Rienninger,	CR	
F. Reinhardt,	⊣R	
do.	F	
Phillip Schafer,	2l	
Geo. Sailzer,	E5	
Phillip J. Wahl,	5O	
Julius Hirshleber,	Hx	
Conrad Wenzel,	WL	

COMAL COUNTY.

Name	Brand	Mark
William Sahm,	S)	
Edward Foerster,	EF	
do,	F2	
do.	—F	
Mrs. Martias Haag,	H3	
Andres Pape, jr.	P2	
Leudwig Schutz,	LS	
J. Calhoun,	JC	
C. Hohmann,	Hh	
Sylvester Simon,	YS	
Thomas Schwab,	HS	

COMAL COUNTY. 153

Miss. Annie Bremer,	⍭	
Miss. E. & A. Bremer,	←HB	
Geo. Appman,	⍝B	
do.	AR	
F. L. H. Coering,	∈	
E. Ben. George,	G7	
Michael Haseldanz,	H3	
George Ullrich,	GU	
Wm. Ullrich,	U	
Th. Diesselhorst,	D	
Carl Schaefer,	⌼	

COMAL COUNTY.

Name	Brand	Mark
Jacob Schmidt,	JS	
Nichola Zurcher,	NZ	
Christian Busch,	B (in shield)	
Mrs. Maria Schmidt,	F	
Henry Bitter,	HB	
do.	W	
Henry Startz.	Y	
Gustave Artz,	CA	On right side
Ign Wenzel	⚓-like symbol	
T. B. Hoffman,	⚓	
Valentine Schwab,	VS	

COMAL COUNTY.

Name	Brand	Mark
Heuriech Heitkamp,	⋋H⋌	⬭
Adam Schlader,	⑦⑤	
do.	75	
H. Twiefel,	ŦL	⬭
Jacob Weilbacher,	OZ	⬭
Jacob Heidrech,	JH	⬭
Christian Loffler,	←L	⬭
Carl Schuchart,	C͡S	⬭
C. L. Hilger,	JR	⬭
Christian Kneeiper,	K⚲	⬭
Peter Kneeiper.	PF ⬭ *⬭	

COMAL COUNTY.

Mathias Uhr,	⌢⌢ (oo)	
Conrad Pape, jr.	ʃ	⊂⊃
Wm. Pape,	℞	⊂⊃
H Uhr,	UR	⊂⊰
do *	⊢U	⊂⊃
Louis Vogle,	V	⊱⊃
L. Weitzfelder,	ⵏF	●⊰
do.	✿	
do. *	WD	●⊰
Jacob Katerlie,	Ju	⊱●
Carl George,	C G	⊂⊰

COMAL COUNTY 157

Peter Horne,	PH	⊂⊃ * ⊂⊃
Valentine Fei,	VF	⊂⊃
G. Burckhardt,	GB	⊂⊃
Martin Simon,	SN	⊂⊃
Phillip Jones,	PJ	⊂⊃
Mrs. Anna Syring,	CS	⊂⊃
do. *	CS	⊂⊃
Miss. Anna Winkler,	W	⊂⊃
P. Markwardt,	JM	⊂⊃
do. *	DM	⊂⊃
A. L. Bueshe,	A	⊂⊃

158 COMAL COUNTY.

Name	Brand	Mark
Heinrich Barbe,	B	
J. J. Haas,	3	
August Haas,	C H	
Joseph Hirholzer,	JZ	
Adam Wuest,	S AW	
Andres Gass,	GS	
Mrs. C. Bielstien,	HZ	
Phillip Wagner,	WA	
Henry Kraft,	KT	
Fredrick Toll,	FT	

H. Kublemacher,	K2	
B. F. Smithson,	S—	
do.	—S	
George Pfeuffer,	GP	
Henry Busch,	HB	
Carl Uhr,	7U	
do.	40	
Jacob Stahl,	41	
Gotlebe Artz,	CA	On left side
Mrs. M. H. Smith,	⋂	
J. John,	ℬ	

C. Hofheinz,	Ƕ	ↄ⊃
S. Tanner,	T	⊂ↄ

COMAL RANCHO P. O.

Diederiech Voges.	DV	⊇⊃
J. T. Toler.	T	⊂⊃
John Carson,	JC	⊇⊃
Chas. Power	ⵂL	⊂⊃⊂⊙⊃
Dutrich Knibbe,	ⵂK	⊂⊃
J. M. Secrest,	○+	⊂⊐
do.	D	⊂⊐
do.	F	

COMAL COUNTY

Name	Brand	Mark
Sebastian Beierle,	SB	
do.	*BS	
Hans Specht.	OOO	
Gabriel Remmlar,	CR	
Sebastian Schertz,	Z	
Charles Scheft,	♉	
do.	CS	
do.	*CS	
Miss M. Diets,	TIL	
Jacob Seegers,	8 J	

COMAL COUNTY.

Fredrick Reest,	ℬ	◐◑
do.	R	◐◯
Charles Esser,	S A	϶϶
do.	A	϶϶
George Krause,	4K	⊃϶ * ⊂⊃
Charles Akermann,	AX	⊃⊂
Valentine Fuhrmann,	5F	϶϶
O. M. Secrest.	L7	
E. Q. Krugener,	EK	▷⊃
Henry Imhoff,	J+F	◐⊃

LIVE OAK CO. Oakville P. O.

Alexander Coker,	∧C	
W. T. C. Butler,	—C	
do.	55	
J. R. Williams,	◉	
Wm. McIntosh,	MC	
do.	JN	
do.	22	
Mrs. McIntosh,	ᒪ JJ	
Curtis Herring,	B	

LIVE OAK COUNTY.

J. E. Gildea or Agt.,	IDA	⊂⊃
do.	4	
W. Minter	MI	⊂⊃
do.	OJ	
J. R. Bartlett,	80	⊂⊃
Sebastian Bell,	SB	⊂⊃
do.	BS (inverted)	
Mrs. E. C. Goodwin,	DO	⊂⊃
do.	CO	
W. Williams,	(K	⊂⊃

LIVE OAK COUNTY. 165

John Williams,	⌒J	
Thos. Pugh,	TP	
B. Pugh,	BP	
T. R. Harrison,	SU	
John Healy,	CH	
R. B. Johnson,	JJ	
P. F. Shipp,	◇	
A. B. Dodson.	SD	
E. Votaw,	VO	
do.	*V	

LIVE OAK COUNTY.

Name	Brand	Mark
J. T. Herritage or Agt.,	TW	
do.	J⊃	
do.	J	
Michael Oheny,	M	
Albert Butler,	2B	
Henderson Waller,	JW	
R. Tullous,	R	
M. V. Edes,	y	
Z. H. Osborn,	⊖S	
Walter Meriman,	◇	*
Louis C. Latham,	IT	

LIVE OAK COUNTY.

Wm. Pugh,	PE	
do.	WP	
James Harrison,	HP	
P. C. Brenan,	PB	
do.	JP	
G. W. Frazier,	IXL	
do.	GF	
do.	ZX	
M. M. Dodson,	ND	
do.	SD	
Bymum & Ferrell,	BF	

LIVE OAK COUNTY.

L. Smith,	O	(ear marks)
do.	L S	
do.	S W	
do.	*B Y	
Mrs. M. Ferrell,	W F	
Henderson Williams,	O H	(ear marks)
do.	Ł	(ear marks)
J. G. King,	G K	(ear marks)
do.	*J K	(ear marks)
do.	*U B	(ear marks)
S. S. McWhorter,	ſ	(ear marks)

LIVE OAK COUNTY. 169

Henry Taylor,	HT	
do.	HT	
do.	III	
do.	Y	
Waller Slorter,	WS	
do. *	J	
Thos. Wilburn,	TW	
John Ellis,	9	
G. W. Wright,	6	
James Latham,	L6	
Jas. R. Latham,	L6	

LIVE OAK COUNTY.

Name	Brand	Earmark
John Latham,	LL	
Alfred Robinson,	AR	*
do. *	JR	
J. E. Stephens,	JM	
do.	JM	
Mathew Kinlin,	BK	
do.	K	
James Murray,	K	
H. F. Chambles,	HFC	
John Chambles,	JL	
do.	JL	

LIVE OAK COUNTY.

Name	Brand	Mark
M. C. Chambles,	F9P	⊖⊙
J. H. Dalton,	T53	
Mrs. Ann J. Hinton,	JTP	⊙⊖
Samuel Bell,	⌒O⌒	⊖⊙
do.	œ	⊖⊙
Edwin D. Crow,	CRO	⊖⊙
do.	*27	⊖⊙
do.	2C	
Sam. Mass,	SM	⊖⊙
J. W. Drury or Agt.	JD	⊖⊙

H. B. Newberry,	HN	
C. W. Newberry,	LN	
J. C. Newberry,	2O	
John Marshall,	⚏	
do.	12	
Mathew Givens,	A2	
do.	A2	
Hunter & Cox,	HC	
C. C. Cox,	6x	
Wm. Gambel,	WG	

GUSSETVILLE P. O.

Robert Daugherty,	RD	
H. J. O'Reily,	HR	⊖⊃
Thos. Shannon,	TS	⊖⊃
James Dolan,	JD	⊖⊃
John R. Francis,	F	⊂⊃
Mrs. M. Nichols.	NOT	⊖⊃
do.	*NO	
Thos. Sheeren,	SIX	⊕⊃
Patrick Gallagher,	AT	⊖⊃
do.	A̤T̤ ♡	

Miss Jo. Gusset,	NG	
S. W. Lewis,	SL	
do.	⊥S	
P. Pugh,	P	
do.	P	
M. Dolan,	MD	
Mrs. E. Dolan,	ED	
Pat Dolan,	PD	
Thos. Dolan,	JD	
John Dolan,	HE	
B. Gallagher,	BS	

Patrick Fox,	FOX	
do.	DF	
Thos. Gallagher,	TAX	⊃⊂
J. W. Rainey,	R̂	⊂⊃
Mrs. Mary Sheeran,	PS	⊃⊂
do.	OS	⊂⊃
Patrick Sheeran,	PAT	⊃⊂
Mrs. Margret Evans.	NG	

ECHO P. O.

Jas. M. Grovers,	Mc
Wm. Clark,	PJ

G. Z. Wilson,	Z∧C	
do.	Z	
Mrs. E. C. Wilson,	S	
E. S. Shipp,	A	
do.	S	
S. G. Miller,	M♡	
do.	*♡	
W. W. Stephens,	JR	
do.	JR	

McMULLEN CO. Oakville P. O.

W. J. Kyle,	K̂	⊂⊃ * ⊂⊃
R. A. Brown,	RB	⊃⊃
C. W. Brown.	Ĉ	⊂⊃
do. *	CB	⊂⊃
Mrs. S. A. Brown,	SB	⊂⊃
do.	SB (inverted)	
W. J. Brown,	W B	⊂⊃
M. C. Brown,	M B	⊂⊃
L. D. Yarbrough	D Y	⊂⊃

MCMULLEN COUNTY.

Name	Brand	Mark
A. Yarbrough,	Ⅎ	⊖⊖
do.	D	
Caroline Wimble,	30	⊕⊖
Mrs. L. J. Sparks.	S	⊖⊕
J. D. Walker,	UT	⊖⊖
do.	J36	
do.	3	
S. W. Walker,	36	⊕⊕
W. P. Crain,	ЯF	⊖⊕
A. Franklin,	S̄	⊖⊖

MC MULLEN COUNTY. 179

James Lowe,	H	
do.	H	
do.	AD	
do.	CB	
do.	*AN	
do.	*CI	
R. A. Fountain,	UF	
do.	⊃F	
do.	CF	
Wm. Franklin,	♡W	
G. W. Kennedy,	3K	

J. M. Franklin,	ꟻC	

PLEASENTON P. O.

A. Lane,	LVI	
do.	AL	
W. C. Walker,	ꟻ	
S. Pearce,	J3	
A. Walker,	83	
do.	Æ	

NUECES COUNTY.

CORPUS CHRISTI P. O.

John Dix,   DIX

O. T. Dix,   ⊤DIX

HELENA P. O.

John Rabb.   ⏝⏜   ꓱꓷ

BEXAR CO. San Antonio P. O.

Daniel Devine,	Ⓓ	⋈
J. Q. Adams,	JA	ꟼꓱ
do,	∗JA	ꟼꓱ
do.	∗IOU	ꟼꓳ
do.	∗IK	ꓱꓱ
do.	∗SO	ꟼꓱ ꟼꓱ
do.	∗OXN	ꟼ•ꓳ•ꟼ
Mrs. Sarah Adams,	PA	ꟼꓱ∗ꓱꓱ
do.	∗SPA	ꓱꓱ
Jas. Dunn, Est. of	JD	ꓳ•

BEXAR COUNTY

Name	Brand	Mark
W. H. Jackson,	[J]	(ear marks)
do.	W̄	(ear marks)
J. H. Coker,	[C]	(ear marks)
W. D. Cotton,	WDC	
do.	WDC	
John Wadenpole,	4B	(ear marks)
Joseph Anderson,	ooo	(ear marks)
F. Ujhazy,	ÛL	
do.	UL	
George Knight,	W̄	(ear marks)
Dan. Murphy,	CM	

J.hn James,	IO	⊖⊙
do.	OI	
do.	TEN	
do.	m	
do.	m	
Theo. Heermann & Bro.,	⊤H̶O	
Edwardo Rives,	⌐R	⊙⊖
Jesus Hernandez sr.	(figure)	⊖⊙
Jesus Hernandez,	(figure)	⊖⊙
Ignacio Penna,	⊤P	⊖⊙

BEXAR COUNTY. 185

Name	Brand	Mark
John Bowen,	B	
J. Beze,	B	
W. B. Jaques,	D	
do.	◇	
Jacob Linn,	JL	
J. L. Truehart,		
John Twoig,	JT	
E. C. Dewey,	IOI	
J. A. Settle,	JAS	
P. C. Taylor,	PT	
John C. French,	Æ	

BEXAR COUNTY.

Name	Brand	Mark
W. Lange,	(crown)	
Anton Wottley,	A	
Celestin Jecker,	J2	
Sam'l McCulloch,	9	
Henry Ellermann,	HE	*
Peyton Smythe,	OS	
A. N. Dauchey	5	
James Weir,	⋛	
I. A. Paschal.	◇P	
Manuel Herrera sr.	H	
Blas Herrera jr.	H	

BEXAR COUNTY.

Name	Brand	Mark
Benito Herrera,	⌐P	
Blas Herrera sr.,	H	
H. L. Thompson,	Y C	
do.	ƎW	
do. *	BW	
C. G. Edwards,	CE	
do. *	E	
J. C. Stanfield,	◇ ◇	
W. J. Mitchell,	⌣⌣	
Frank Mitchell,	JO	
S. L. Stanfield,	SL	

BEXAR COUNTY.

J. T. Quesenberry,			
A. W. Desmuke,			
Harrison Presnall,			
do.	*		
John Long,			
do.	*		
Terry O'Neal,			
do.	*		
do.	*		
do.	*		
do.	*		

BEXAR COUNTY.

Name	Brand	Mark
G. Pendleton,	III	
Ignacio Peres,	♃	
Juan Rodriguez,	NR	
Francisco A. Ruiz,	FR	
Eugenio Ruiz.	R	
Manuel Leal,	A	
Sebastian Ripstein,	◇R	
do.	Y On Jaw	
Simon Casanoa,		
R. Casanoa,	L	

BEXAR COUNTY.

Name	Brand	Mark
George Mushall,	OP	
Sampson Coker,	K	
Jacob Gembler,	IG	
John Flanakin,	F2	
do. *	I2	
Bethel Coopwood,	C	On neck.
Ransom Capps,	BOB	
do.	RC	
John Kublemaker,	K	
Gotleb Obst,	OBST	
August Piper,	AP	

BEXAR COUNTY.

Name	Brand	Mark
Henrich Voges,	V G	∞
W. B. Knox,	nOX	
Owings & Knox,	O22	⊂⊃
do.	?	⊂⊃
L. S. Owings,	Z	
F. Herff,	⊁	⊜⊇
J. G. Ward,	JW	⊂⊃⊂⊃
do.	P	⊂⊃
Joseph Coker,	JC	⊜⊇
D. W. Bennett,	DI	⊂⊃
Antono Horn,	⑧	⊜⊃

A. D. Jones,	ADJ	⊖⊕
do. ✲	St ⊖⊃	⊖⊃
S. R. Taylor,	ST	
do. ✲	ST (inverted)	
Geo. McDona,	7O	
Henson & Bro.,	⬡H⬡	
Albert Stow,	STO	C⊃
E. W. Stow,	STO₁	C⊃
Abel Stow,	STO₂	C⊃
A. P. Stow,	STO₃	C⊃

BEXAR COUNTY. 193

Levi Stow,	S T O / 4	
H. W. Stow,	S T O / 7	
Merritt Stow,	S T O / 8	
Geo. H. Noel,	PL	
C. S. Harris,	C̄H̄	
Mrs. E. Dwyer,	Ǝ	
Jose Dionisio Martinez,	M	
Manuel Gil,	A	
Emile Raux,	⟨figure⟩	

Margarita Diaz,		
Pedro Tegeda,		
Juana M. de los Santos,		
Antonio Areola,		
Guadalupe Diaz,		
Romana Herrera,		
Francisco Trevenio,		
Pedro Espinosa,		

BEXAR COUNTY.

Name	Brand	Mark
Jose Maria Herrera,		
Anicoto Martinez,		
Matias Carillo,		
Isabel Carillo,		
Gustave Toudouze,		
Maria de Jesus Castillo,		
Leandro Garcia,		
Dario Castillo,		
Albert Hubert,		
Catarino Rodriguez,		

Domingo Losoyo,		
Jose Alameda,		
Manuel Herrera sr.		
Casimiro Casillas,		
Agapo Bargas,		
Mary A. White,		
David Reynolds,		
Marcelo Casillas,		
Juan M. Gallardo,		

Name	Brand	Mark
Bruno Ortiz,		
F. Herrera de Valdez,		
Francisco Valdez.		
Romano Zuniga,		
Juana F. Diaz,		
Bibian Huron,		
Con McMullegan,		
do.		
Peter Hernandez sr.		

Peter Hernandez jr.	PH	
Anastacio Salines,	XL	
I. P. Simpson,	(symbol)	On horses only.
C. W. Gillis,	YO	
do.	(symbol) *	On cattle only.
do.	(pitcher symbol) *	
M. Gillis,	PN	
Mrs. E. Gillis,	ƎC	
T. L. Odom,	OD	
A. J. Leslie,	⌐	

BEXAR COUNTY 199

A. L. Cashell,	46	
E. B. & S. B. Pue,	15	
do.	*V D	
do.	*10	
do.	*JH	
do.	*T	
do.	*BUL	
Henry Fest,	R̂	
do.	*LF	
Adolph Schurig,	HS	
Christian Werner,	GW	

Name	Brand	Mark
Andre Kuntz,	A2	
Sebastian Kuntz,	KS	
Joseph Weber,	ℛ	
Gregoria Herman.	P	
Chas. Metzdorff,	KM	
Francis Brandy,	BD	
C. F. Kaiserling,	CK	
do.	CK	
E. Buchetti,	CL	
do.	BT	

BEXAR COUNTY.

Joseph Jaegly,	JU	
Charles Power,	H	
Luciano Navarro,	AV	
Jose Martinez,	←L	
do.	NP	
do.	3 On jaw.	
R. M. Smith,	RS	
Joseph Smith,	JS	
Christian Gembler,	96	
W. A. Weatherby,	⟨V⟩	
M. M. Childers,	2	

BEXAR COUNTY.

T. P. Dashiel,	4 4	
do.	HK	
do.	Y	
do.	MD	
do.	DHD	
do.	FEM	
do.	JX	
do.	JYD	
Charles Miller,	♡	
do.	my	
Jesus Zapada,	ℛ	

BEXAR COUNTY.

E. Tynan,	ET	(brand)
do.	ƎKT	
do.	*TE	(brand)
do.	*▷D	(brand)
Geo. W. Mudd,	MUD	(brand)
do.	U5	(brand)
W. P. Kerr,	∩	(brand)
W. H. Kerr,	(I)	(brand)
do.	*KR	(brand)
Mrs. N. R. S. Kerr,	ŌY	(brand)
do.	ŌT	(brand)

J. N. Kerr,	Z	
J. W. DeVilbiss,	D	
J. S. Gillett,	TOP	
do.	*O	
Joseph Beitle,	JB	
do.	*☆	
F. J. Beitle,	IB	
do.	*⌽	
C. F. Beitle,	╫B	
G. Van Riper	V	
E. A. Neighbors Est. of	N̂	

BEXAR COUNTY.

Neighbors & Serna,	NS	
J. F. Serna,	IS	
P. Sarran	SP	
R. B. Campbell,	RBC	
L. Campbell,	LC	
James Huebner,	JU	
C. Hopfelt,	HP	
Barney Mitchell,	BM	
do.	DR	
E. K. Rhodes,	R	
do.	R	

BEXAR COUNTY.

T. A. Smith,	IP	
D. M. Poor.	oLP	
F. S. Poor,	oLI	
Modest Torres,	R	
do.	R	
do.	CT	
do.	AT	
do.	NR	
do.	ʓ	
do.	☆	

BEXAR COUNTY.

Name	Brand	Mark
Theo. Knight,		
J. R. Cloud,	JC	
H. A. Langwell,	H₃	
Jose Antonio de la Garcea,		
Jose McGil de la Garcea,		
G. F. Marnoch,	M	
do.	A	
R. H. Belvin,	⊙	
do.	33	
Z. Van Ward,	EW	
J. McCann,	CAN	

BEXAR COUNTY.

Name	Brand	Mark
Nat. Lewis,	NO	
do.	ON	
Sol. C. Childress.	D	
do.	ՆB	
Polk & Sam Childress,	PS	
T. F. Corry,	IV-	
do.	※ IV	
Asa Mitchell,	∩	
J. J. Durler,	↻	
T. G. Gardner	TGG	
Charles Lege.	⚲	

Jose Maria Rodriguez,	SM	
Francisco Menjares,	FM	
Salome Valdes,	⚭	⊖◡
T. Grayson,	SIS	⊖◡
do.	MC	⊂◦◦
do.	JMC	⊂◦◦
do.	MC	⊖◡
do.	2R	◦⊂◡
Albert Urbahn,	AU	⊖◡
Alejandro M. Ruiz,	R	⊖◡

BEXAR COUNTY.

Antonio Lombrana,	NL	
Lewis W. Nuckolls,	JN	
do.	⁎ ⌒⌒	
James M. Bright,	N	
James M. Smith, jr.	7	
W. R. Park,	7T	
D. C. Ogden,	D O	
Mrs. J. C. Wood,	Hh	
Jesse Applewhite,	UC	
A. J. Lackey,	J7	

BEXAR COUNTY

	Brand	Mark
B. B. Gayle,	∈	
W. C. Newton,	SA	
James M. Fisk,	⟨F⟩	
do.	ÆF	
do.	(figure)	
Seaman Field,	H̵	
do.	SF	
E. D. Lane,	EDL	
do.	*EL	
do.	*ŌK	

BEXAR COUNTY.

S. C. Thompson,	DN	CD
Anton Schreier,	ÂS	CD
William Vance,	Ŭ	
Christian Schleyer,	⬠	CD
G. H. Buechsenschuetz,	1̄6̄	CD
G. Schleicher,	GUS	CD
do.	SC	
Albert Moye,	m	CD
John Kenny,	▽T	CD
do.	SK	[CD

BEXAR COUNTY.

Thos. Kenny,	TK	
Peter Gallagher,	JR	
Peter & Ed. Gallagher,	G	
Jesse Jones,	▢ On left hip. ℘ On right hip.	
do.	* ℘	
F. Briggs,	VD	
do,	VD	
J. A. Forbes,	A	
do.	⊕	
J. C. Bacon,	JB	

BEXAR COUNTY.

Name	Brand	Earmark
E. B. Bacon,	♣	
George Hoerner,	CH	
J. G. Geiser,	2 × I	
W. G. Kingsburry,	K̂	
Christian Gembler,	9G	
G. Jagge,	♃	
Wm. Ucker,	FU	
Jacob Goll	GJ	
Wm. Fink,	F̂	
Anton Lorenz.	AT / I	

BEXAR COUNTY. 215

Name	Brand	Mark
Mrs. J. Jeffries,	Ĵ	
W. Jeffries,	Ⓦ	
G. T. Howard,	TH	
do.	THD	
S. C. Jones,	JOJ	
Aug. Bering,	BL	
E. Mondragon,	EM	
do.	JS	
Francis Mondragon,	Y	
Benito Lopez,	BL	
Mrs. Charlotte Jones,	EJ	

BEXAR COUNTY.

Name	Brand	Mark
Josiah Cass,	CA2	⊖⊃
Placido Olivera,	P O	⊂⊇
S. J. Barker,	26̄	⊖⊇
G. A. Barker,	T V	⊙⊇
A. J. Avent,	U̲	⊂⊇
F. M. Avent,	4 O	⊂⊋
E. B. Pue,	⌒U	⊂⊇
S. B. Pue,	N 5	⊂⊇
Patrick McClusky,	ↄO	⊂⊇
do.	*PY	

Name	Brand	Ear Mark
Mrs. M. Lackey,	M	
Maria Saufrosa Ruiz,	六	
Amos Harris,	LA ∞ ∞ * ∞	
J. Pancoast,	JP	
L. W. Johnson,	7X	
Johnson & McDaniel,	XE	
do.	*MO	
do.	*4E	
Mrs. Cynthia Johnson,	J• On left h'p,	
Virgil Johnson,	T	
W. D. Johnson,	J• On right hip,	

BEXAR COUNTY.

Name	Brand	Earmark
H. C. Johnson,	X6	
Miss M. A. Johnson,	X4	
J. M. Adams,	PD	
do.	*PD	
P. S. Gatman,	15	
Mrs. Lucinda Walters,	W	
A. A. Ackerman,	IA	
C. Uurban,	U	
do.	B	
E. Toole,	HT	
James Smith.	S	

BEXAR COUNTY.

Name	Brand	Notes
Arthur Dillon,	dM	
G. H. Giddings,	GHG	
do.	ℬ	
Adams & Lytle,	I X L	On horses only.
Wm. Lytle,	L	
John Epp,	EP	
do.	FU	
Mrs. E. A. Drown,	D N	
M. L. Merick,	I I I	
John Haw,	RS	
Benjamin Varga,	BV	

John Doblin,	JD (with arc over)
C. G. Krempkau,	+CK
G. B. Torrey,	GBT
Emanuel Rzeppa,	ER
Matilda Rzeppa,	RE
Arter Crownover,	C2
S. S. Womble,	S S
Owen Clark,	OW
S. S. Sampson,	S S

H. J. Inselmann,	T5	
John G. Inselmann,	FJ	
T. S. Jones,	YJ	

CASTROVILLE P. O.

Joseph Meyer,	↓	
Leonhart Hans,	LO	
Edwin Trimble,	L2.	
Mrs. Mary S. Trimble,	T9	
A. & E. Cagnion,	A	
Fritz Zimili,	INO	

BEXAR COUNTY.

Jacob Zimili,	INO	⊂⊃*⊂⊃
do.	Z8	⊂⊃*⊂⊃
J. B. Burrell,	Ƌ	⊂⊃
do.	HO	⊂⊃
John L. Mann,	M	⊃⊂⊃⊂⊃
Jacob Burrell,	65	⊝⊝
do.	ᒐ	⊝⊝
Valentine Mann,	☂	⊡⊡
F. A. Boehme,	⟨B⟩	⊂⊃
John Jungmann,	⊃‖	
Martin Becker,	M3	

Isaac Hutchison,	IH	
O. P. Hutchison;	OP	
W. C. Hutchison,	OU	
Joseph Keller,	JK	
Jacob Sittre,	SI	
Jose ph Sittre,	S	
J. H. Brown,	B	
W. Luckey,	I6	
C. Sattleben jr.	CN	
C. Sattleben sr.	CS	

BEXAR COUNTY.

F. Xavera Young,	⌂4	⊂⊃
James M. Smith sr.	JS	⊂⊃
Mrs. Lucinda Smith,	87	⊂⊃
do.	*WG	⊙⊙
do.	3̄	
do.	*3	
Mrs. Eliza Pearce,	⌂P	
Eliza Ann Jasper,	U U	⊂⊃
J. G. Trimble,	AD	
F. Werzbach.	W̱	⊂⊃

BEXAR COUNTY.   225

Jacob Droitcourt,	JD	
do.	CL	*
Joseph Krticzka sr.		
Joseph Krticzka jr.		
Wilhelm Stuckler,	CAT	
Carl Kieser;	CK	
do.	CK	
Adolph Wurzbach,		
do.	FI	
Herndon & Kerr,	JK	

15

BEXAR COUNTY.

Name	Brand	Mark
J. H. Herndon or Agt.	H	
Julius Wurzbach,	JS	
Seraphim Meyer,	S9	
Sebastian Marty,	S11	
Peter Heineman,	A	

GRAYTOWN P. O.

Name	Brand	Mark
Juan Rodriguez,	R	
Antonio Seguin,	Y	
Joaquin Tarin,	PT	
Mrs. S. Gray,	SG	

BEXAR COUNTY. 227

James Gray,		
William Gray,		
Mrs. Acmonia Gray,		
Miss Mary Gray,		
John S. Shely,	SH	
Antonio Montez,		
Manuel Montez,		
Alejos Montez,		

BEXAR COUNTY.

LEON SPRINGS P. O.

Max Aue,	M (stylized)	⊖⊖
do.	AUE	⊖⊖
H. C. King,	⚒ (square & compass with G)	⊂⊃
do.	G	⊂⊃
H. Haberman,	EH	⊂⊃
G. W. Clark,	♡C	⊖⊖
do.	/H	
do.	JO	
Antone Byer,	⌄B	⊙⊙

BEXAR COUNTY.

Name	Brand	Mark
Geo. Plehwe,	GP	
do.	M	
Fredrick Kraut,	FK	
Anton Gugger,	GK	
Henry M. Smith,	?16	
do	△S	
Johan Vogt,	HV	
P. S. Oatman,	15	
G. W. Maltsburger,	♡	

SELMA P. O.

Name	Brand	Ear Mark
J. B. Brown,	◇B	
Wm. Davenport,	WD	
William Geier,	WC	
Martin Schmed,	M / S	
John G. Miller,	KM	
do.	/FS	
do.	UF	
do.	⊢C	
do.	⊕	

J. B. Fonda,	⊐F⌐	
Adolph Real.	88	
Mrs. Rhoda Lann,	JL	⊖⊖
Miss Sarah F. Lann,	JL S K	J L, on shoulder. S K, on side. ⊖⊖
Miss Minerva L. Lann,	⌐⌐	⊖⊖
Mrs. A. P. A. T. Park,	P	⊂⊃
Smith & Hale,	SH	⊂⊃
W. O. Hines,	FOX	⊂⊃
W. A. Hale,	◁|▷	
E. C. Hines,	◇	⊂⊃

Robt. Weir,	RW	⊖⊃
R. B. Evans,	ℬ	⊂⊙⊃

VALLEY P. O.

R. W. Brahan,	◁B ⊖⊃ * ⊖⊃	
T. T. Cunningham Est of	TCᴜ	⊂⊃
do.	* ⌒	
do.	* B͡B	
do.	♃	
do.	⌢P	
do.	* ◇	⊂⊃

BEXAR COUNTY. 233

John Miller,		
Edward Stapper,		
John S. McGee,		
do.		
J. B. Ewell,		
J. M. Trainer,		
W. L. Hawkins,		

GUADALUPE CO. New Braunfls P. O.

Name	Brand	Mark
M. Keopsel,	MK	
Wm. Zuhl,	WZ	
Christopher Monk,	B	
Fredrick Baker,	4B	
Carl Schulz,	SO	
Christian Grimm,	CG	
John Nagle,	JN	
Wm. Thiele,	℘	
F. Rudeleff,	FR	
John Zipp,	JZ	

Aug. Pfannstiel,	ÆL	CO
Wm. Pfannstiel,	ÆL	CO
Aug. Weyel,	AW	⊖⊃
Henreeh Kurre,	♡	⊖⊃
John Schnabel,	SL	⊖⊃
do.	RO	⊖⊃
Aug. Ebert,	AE	◊◊
Michael Schulz,	MS	⊖⊃
Aug. Bauer,	AB	CO
J. H. Schultze,	2S	CO
L. H. Hoffman,	HE	CO

John Orth,	HO	
Fredrick Eberling,	FE	
Conrad Voges,	HV	
do.	IV	
Carl Krueger,	✳	
Jacob Orth,	♂	
Conrad Engelke,	CE	
Christopher Koehler,	KO	
Gustave Altwein.	ƆAC	
Thomas Day,	Ŧ	
John F. Hoffman,	(reversed 6)	

GUADALUPE COUNTY. 237

Peter Hoffman,	P9	
Henrich Hoffman,	5 Ⓗ	
Frank Reinhard,	J3	
T. A. Blumberg,	B6	
Wm. Knetsch,	WK	
Wm. Schulz,	WS	
Valentine Klein,	VK	
Fredrick Ernst,	SL	
C. Maurer,	AM	
Wm. Bartels,	B / W	

GUADALUPE COUNTY.

Name	Brand	Mark
George Hild,	4	
do.	CH	
Fredrick Pfannstiel,	P X	
Mrs Margaret Molberg,	CM	
Carl Hutmacher,	SH	
Jasper Gelven,	∏ G	
F. D. Pfannstiel,	P	
do.	* P	
Ludwig Kurre,	ℒ K	
Mrs. M. J. Acker,	AKR	
Henry Grobe,	ҺG	

GUADALUPE COUNTY.

Name	Brand	Mark
Henry Scheler,	HSh	
Mrs. Sophia Schraub,	J JS	
do.	A SC	
do.	E SC	
do.	N SC	
Phillip Schraub,	P SC	
Mrs. Catharine Asher,	EK	
Fredrick Zuhl,	C Z	
Earnst Linne,	E L	
Carl Rathke,	R	
C. R. Elly,	E Y	

GUADALUPE COUNTY.

B. Schneider,	S	(marks)
do.	ML	
Johannette Leihner,	ML / L	(marks)
Henry Wiedner,	HW	(marks)
do.	H / F	(marks)
Henry Geske,	HG	(marks)

SELMA P. O.

Morris Ferris,	NF	(marks)
do.	F	(marks)

GUADALUPE COUNTY.

Burrel Lann,	BL	
John Young,	Y	
W. J. Young,	WY	
Mrs. O. Rhodius,	HR	
do.	☆	

VALLEY P. O.

M. Amacher,	AA	
Fred. Sassmannhausen,	34	
Wm. Seiler,	⊣S	
Jacob Seiler.	⊢S (reversed)	

GUADALUPE COUNTY.

Name	Brand	Mark
Robt. Hellmann,	⊕	
Christopher Beller,	CB	
Jacob Pfeil,	P.F	
Wm. R. Elam,	RE	
do.	*JW	
A. G. Goodloe,	UB	
do.	*UB	
Fred. Vordenbaumen,	FU	
Wm. S Hamilton,	MHL	
do.	WH	

GUADALUPE COUNTY.

Name	Brand	Mark
John Wetz,	W	
J. H. Burruss,	HB	
J. P. Meurin,	MR	
Mrs. D. Brotze,	B	
C. Brotze,	R	
Otto Brotze,	OZ	
T. J. Perryman,	TP	
Christian Schneider,	ABC	
Miss Helena Seiler,	HS	
H. P. Young,	YG	

GUADALUPE COUNTY.

J. G. Bergfeld,	BF	
do.	V On jaw	
Ferdinand Dietz,	DIZ	
Carl Conrad,	GC	
do.	*HC	
Fred. Eahl,	FE	

SEGUIN P. O.

H. A. Dugger,	ID On left hip — A On right	
Mrs. C. A. Gilispie,	13	
Riley Lewis,	R	

GUADALUPE COUNTY. 245

A. H. Rhodes,	UC	
Joseph Wilson,	5	C●
Dudley Tom,	WT C● * C	
do.	DT	C
William Tom,	WT C * C	
Geo. A. Tom,	6I	C
John Brooks,	J2	C
Sanford Brown,	♀	C
do.	I5	C●
M. H. Reynolds,	7D	E
Patrick Lyons,	45	●C

GUADALUPE COUNTY.

Wm. Saffold,	S	⊂⊃*⊂⊃
Watkins V. Mays,	M3	⊂⊃
Mrs Anna D. Mays,	JM	⊂⊃
Evans' heirs,	⏋	⊂⊃
Charles Wather,	†/W	⊂⊃
John R. Anderson,	X	⊂⊃
W. C. Morrison,	H̄	⊂⊃
Ed. H. Williams,	EW	⊃⊃
Mrs. Sarah Irvin,	A	⊃⊃
W. C. Irvin,	A On side	C On hip ⊃S

GUADALUPE COUNTY.

Mrs Martha Campbell,	JT	
John Campbell,	WF	
do.	Jo	

SUTHERLAND SPRINGS P. O.

Ben. Goodwin,	℧E	
do.	BEN	
Mrs. S. R. Henderson,	JH	
J. H. Polley,	JP	
J. B. Polley,	SP	
Jacob Miller,	13 on left shoulder	M on right.

GUADALUPE COUNTY.

LAVERNIA P. O.

Name	Brand	Mark
D. C. Newton,	⊤ (with cross)	
James Newton,	JN on one side, + Opposite	
do.	⁎ 69	
do.	⁎ OO	
J. F. Tiner,	JF	
J. A. Wells,	▭	
James Humphries,	JH	
Mrs. Elizabeth Applewhite,	5	
Wm. Morris,	WM	
do.	R	

GUADALUPE COUNTY 249

R. W. Morris,

E. A. Barker,

do. Horses on thigh, Mares on hip.

E. C. Barker,

PRAIRIE LEA P. O.

D. A. Ward,

DEWITT CO. Yorktown P. O.

Name	Brand	Mark
W. J. McKinney,	TK	
Jonathan York,	YL	
do.	12	
J. W. Faris,	JF	
Wm. E. Couch	28	
Jack H. Friar,	JF	
Mrs Elizabeth Taylor,	WT	Shoulder horses – Hip cattle
Miss E. J. Taylor,	WT	Hip horses – Shoulder cattle.
Wm. B. Taylor,	W2	

DEWITT COUNTY.

251

Name	Brand	Mark
Joseph Taylor,	J5	
John M. Taylor,	J3	
Justus Odom,	O5	
Mrs. Martha Odom,	JO	
Mrs. Caroline Hains,	C y	
M. Fleming,	ⓕ	
Miss M. J. Fleming,	JD	
do,	*JC	
M. A. Harper,	MH	
do.	E2	
Mrs. Hariet A. For?,	F	

DEWITT COUNTY.

Name	Brand	Mark
Walter Anderson,	OA	
Richmond Anderson,	OSO	
David Murray,	8S	
W. B. Praytor,	7P	
do.	*53	
S. Brown,	SB	
Mrs. Mary Lambert,	IB	
W. R. Russell,	NC	
Mrs. Isabella Woods,	M	
J. Afflerbach,	VI	
Julius Gohmert,	GC	

DEWITT COUNTY.

Name	Brand	Mark
Fredrick Rummel,	FR	
Louis Sasse,	2S	
Joseph Tumlinson,	23	
do.	2	
J. J. Tumlinson,	2-0	
L. B. Wright,	22	
J. T. Kilgore,	φ	
do.	JK	
Henry Mahust,	X3	
Vincent Zowada,	Z	
Freid, Pritz,	P7	

DEWITT COUNTY.

Name	Brand	Earmark
Mrs. R. Peace,	HP	
Wm. Aaron,	A6	
Louis Kroschel,	CK	
do.	*CL	
Fred Gohlke.	⑤	
do.	WIL	
do.	MIN	
Ludwig Klotz,	LK	
E. M. Edwards,	Ǣ	
Frantz Hoppe,	JF	
Andrew Strirber,	St	

DEWITT COUNTY.

Name	Brand	Mark
Wm. Duerr,	D5	
Charles Galle,	XG	
Peter Kilbasa	&K	
Peter Gerhardt,	PG	
Chas. Gerhardt,	KC	
Houston Powel,	HF	
Mrs. E. J. Haruff,	H5	
Mrs. Phœbe Willburn,	W	
Wm. R. Rattliff,	JT	
Geo. W. Jacobs,	GJ	
M. Peace,	M P	

Name	Brand	Mark
John Schneider,	S	
Aug. Westphal,	AW	
do.	TV	
Mrs. Ant Lundscin,	ᘳI	
Daniel Schneider,	DS	
W. & S. B. Grafton,	工	
A. J. Jacobs,	GJ	
Cæsar Eckhardt,	ϵ E	Cattle on hip Horses shoulder.
Peter Metz.	M	
do.	M+	
do.	M3	

DEWITT COUNTY. 257

Name	Brand	Marks/Location
do.	M4	
Miss L. Metz,	M1	
Miss Amelia Metz,	M2	
Robt. C. Eckhardt,	ΞE	Cattle on right side, horses hip
Wm. Eckhardt,	ΞE	Cattle on left side,
Herman Eckhardt,	[L] G	Cattle on hip, horses shoulder,
Ludwig Reidesel,	LR	
W. Hahn,	H	
M. Riedel,	R	
Miss C. Schaffe,	7S	

DEWITT COUNTY.

Jake Yocum,	J†	
do.	T y	
Fredrick Boldt,	BO	
Adolph Strieber,	St	
David Stauchues,		
Mrs. Mary Koch,		
John G. Gohlke,	GO	
H. Aflerbach,	HA	
Wyatt Auderson,	UD	
Chas. Gaebler,	FG	

DEWITT COUNTY.

Name	Brand	Earmark
Julius Kuast,	P2	
Mrs. Julia Gentsch.	AG	
Heinrch Martin,	H5	
Lebrecht Boldt,	LB	
Bernard Engels,	BE	
Gotlebe Sturher.	SF +	
John Kirlicks,	K1	
Wm. Kirlicks,	K2	
Augst Krage.	AK	
do.	SG	

DEWITT COUNTY.

Name	Brand	Mark
Christopher Kirlicks,	JK3	
Jacob Grun,	JG9	
Walentine Zimon,	ZI	
John Korschal,	125	
Daniel Faris,	DP	
T. J. Faris,	J	
S. M. Yocum,	Ty on hip,	
Fredrick Sasse,	BD	
Chas. Dahlman,	CD	
J. P. Ainsworth,	P	
?. H. Hahn,	4	

DEWITT COUNTY.

Name	Brand	Earmark
Peter Homrighausen,	☿	
Fredrick Buer,	♉B	
F. House,	SF	
L. P. Grun,	JGC	
Charles Strieber,	CSt	
Rinhold Gohlke,	4A	
John Mahurst,	X4	
Mrs. H. Goehring,	T4	
Elijah Ratliff,	△	
David Holdeman,	CH	

Willhelm Zuan,	AJ	
Nicholas Kauffman,	NK	
Mrs. C. Braunig,	FB	
John Treude,	JT	
James W. Faris,	+2	
G. W. Humphreys,	S	
do.	P	
do.	(2	
John F. Gohlke,	FG	
August Goehring,	GG	

Johann Gohlke,	AFG	
do.	120	
do.	217	
Gottliebe Schultz,	HM	
do.	*S4	
Mrs. Justine Gohmert,	Ht on right side,	
Henrech Menn,	Ht on hip,	
Mrs. Louise Korth,	Ht on left side,	
J. V. Roeder,	(flower)	
H. G. Woods,	J	

J. M. Denson,		
do.		
Ludolph Tampke,		
do.		
John Sickor,		
do.		
do.	☆	
do.	H7	
Samuel Powel,		
August Carri,		

DEWITT COUNTY.

Name	Brand	Mark
Mrs. S. F. Fleming,	J̵	
do.	HE	
T. J. Bacley,	2U	
Wm. Schley,	52l	
John Range,	R̥₊	
F. Lempke,	?L	
J. D. Brauiley,	OK	
Antonio Metz.	E	
Joseph Ludwik,	ƐK	
Fredrich Menn,	HM	

C. F. W. Hennig,		
G. Lindscin,		
Geo. Volkel,		
Henry Post,		
John T. Porter,	on hip / opposite.	
do.		
C. H. Heisjig,		
Mrs. Ann Pritz,		
Anastasio Reyes,		
Chas. Wagenschein,		

DEWITT COUNTY. 267

Mrs. Jo. Riedel,	MR	
Chas. Riedel,	KR	
Mrs. M. C. McFarland,	S-S	
Henry Sasse.	CS ⊢⊣	
do.	*¦Ⓛ-	
do.	*L	
Joseph Escalaro,	S-O	
J. M. Borchers,	cM	
D. N. Hardy,	P	
J. N. Frazier,	O-S	
O. H. Bennett,	O-B	

DEWITT COUNTY.

Joseph Riddle,	7R	brands
do.	*7	brand
do.	*MD	brand
Rudolph Gohmert,	97	brands
John Grur,	JG	brand
Mrs. L. Odom,	H5	
W. F. King & Bro.	7L	C

CLINTON P. O.

Wm. M. Wheat	||||	brand
Webb Wofford,	TO	
Joseph N. Heard.	21	C

DEWITT COUNTY.

J. W. Robison,	JR	
L. H. Delony,	DE	
do.	*M	
John M. Bay,	BAY	
H. Heard,	⊕	
George C. Tennille,	8	Horses on shoulder,
S. M. Fuckett,	AS	
John R. Kelso,	J2	
James M. Dow,	DOW	
Alfred Allee,	A	
W. A. Blackwell,	AB	

DEWITT COUNTY

J. M. Bell,	JL	
J. B. Cox,	JX	
Mrs. K. J. Taylor,	7T	
do.	*H	
R. B. White,	KB	
Miss. M. Harrell,	3	
Mrs. Cyrena Caruthers,	⊚	
Fredrick Brown,	J+	
T. J. Tuggl	TJT	
S. D. Calhoun,	◇C◇	

DEWITT COUNT.

Name	Brand	Mark
A. McAlister,	<)	
do.	*V ∧	
George Lord,	⋄	
Mrs. Sarah Epperson,	3A	
Thomas J. Wheat,	U3ΣϾ *ᏮⲦ	
do.	*||||	
do.	*W̄	
W. D. Hearn,	27	
Gustave Holzapfel,	9H	
Joseph M. Smith,	⌡	
do.	*50	

DEWITT COUNTY.

Name	Brand	Mark
A. M. Summers,	A̅S̅	
do.	*AS	
do.	⋀	
Joel B. Heard,	ᵇE	⊂⊃
G. W. Brooks jr.	F	⊂⊃
J. H. Brooks,	K	⊂⊃
G. W. Brooks sr.	B	⊂⊃
Henry Hoffman	3	⊂⊐
D. D. Scrivner	4	⊂⊃
do.	S1	
Fred Kriksi	∠	⊂⊃

DEWITT COUNTY.

H. B. Boston,	D|	
Mrs. C. Webb,	⊤B	
do.	FN	
Jacob Lobel.	⌒VL	
Mrs. Jluia McMillan,	XB	
Robt. Brown,	Jh	
do.	21Λ	
do.	*B	
do.	*2ϒ	
Julius Schorre,	ᛯ	

Wm. Schorlemmer,	Ⓢ	
do.	S	
Ed. Holzapfel,	HE	
do.	HH	
J. H. Richter.	JR	
Jacob Reinhardt,	R	
Louis Tewes,	LT	
Antone Hoffer,	H3	
Ferdinand Rochl,	FR	
A. P. Wheat	R	

DEWITT COUNTY.

275

Name	Brand	Mark
F. B Webb,		
Mrs. A. J. Tennille,		
H. Faber,		
do,		
Mrs. S A. Wofford		
J. R. Hamilton,		
Robt H. Spinks,		
Mrs. E. Warren,		
Robt. Roehl,		
Miss A. E. Murphree,		

Alex. Hamilton,	46	
do.	*JH	
do.	*ĤL	
do.	*JL	
Mrs. S. Tennille,	GT	
Louis Reinhardt	ℬ	
M. Blackwell,	ȱ	
do.	PG	
A. F. Newman.	Aᶦ	

DEWITT COUNTY. 277

MEYERSVILLE P. O.

Name	Brand	Mark
Adolph Meyer,	🏠M	⊂⊃
Robt. Kleberg,	✝	⊂⊃
do.	△	⊂⊃
A. Seitz.	⌒⌒	◁⊃
Ambrose Hans,	|A|	⋈
W. V. Limuber,	vR	⊂⊃
A. F. Bueking,	℔	⋈
Miss T. Winkler,	F͡G	⊂⊃
Mrs. Mary Brown,	MB	⊃⊃

DEWITT COUNTY.

Miss D. E. Brown,	CB	
Gideon Dreier,	E5	
Miss Cath. Golly,	C5	
Fokke Jdeus,	JD	
Mrs. H. Rabke,	RE	
Antonio Ott,	OT	
Nicholas Fuchs,	FU	
F. J. Zengerle,	JZ	
W. C. & C. F. Brown,	C̄	
Moses Ashworth or Agt.		

DEWITT COUNTY.

Name	Brand	Earmark
D. B. Peavy,	3P	
Simon Jdens,	D	
Anton Golly,	GO	
do,	ЯH	
do.	FI	
Nicolas Munch,	MN	
Adolph Haun,	AH	
A. Koenig	K9	
Joseph Grunewald,	C7	
Pantaleon Luder,	LU	
Charles Gentke,	KG	

DEWITT COUNTY.

Joseph Bitterly,	HJ	
Jacob Schiwetz,	JS	
Fredrick Schiwetz,	FV	
Christoph Diebel,	[C]	
do.	18	
Christian Moaller,	CM	
do.	*20	
Peter Rath,	RAT	
W. J. Porter,	S7	
do.	SO	
Anton Hotz,	H	

DEWITT COUNTY. 281

H. Mumbrauer,		
E. N. Burk,		
Adam Sager,		
Jacob Prusky,		
Antoine Kohler,		
F. Duderstat,		
do.		
do.		
Wm. Trautwin,		
do.		
John G. Junker,		

Andres Biehrig,		
Michael Hiller,		
Fredrich Hiller,		
Mrs. C. Thieme,		
do.		
Otto Fuchs,		
James Rives,		
do.		
Ben. Eckhart,		
G. L. Thieme,		
A. Scivers,		

DEWITT COUNTY.

L. F. Mack or agt.		
Mrs. E. H. Taylor,		
Josiah Taylor, Est. of		
Chas. Schafer,		
do.		
do.		
James F. Jones,		

MISSION VALLEY P. O.

Richard Power.		

GOLIAD CO. Goliad P. O.

Name	Brand	Mark
Mrs. M. H. Mellews,	MC	
W. B. Killebrew,	K	
J. H. Greculy,	C7	
Jesse Hord,	36	
Mrs. M. C. Fell,	W3	
do.	3F	
do.	3	
G. W. Killebrew,	GK	
Green Bowen,	⋒	
James L. Stappe,	JS	

GOLIAD COUNTY. 285

F. E. Murry,	WM	
do.	M	
S. R. Linsey,	SL	
J. M. Wright	H-	
Hiram Lunsford,	L	
Y. N. Ludeback,	PI	
do.	PIL	
Charley Middleton,	65	
Robt. Christian,	OS	
W. H. Williams,	W	
John Thigpen	JT	

GOLIAD COUNTY.

Name	Brand	Mark
W. B. Torian.	LX	
do.	*BT	
do.	*HX	
do.	*WBT	
W. S. Torian,	JH	
do.	*LIS	
do.	*73	
Miss F. L. M. Sawyers,	FS	
Caspian Seay,	CS	
Mrs. V. Rush,	PR1	
do.	*PR	
Miss. C. Reynolds,	CR	

GOLIAD COUNTY.

Name	Brand	Mark
Peter Rush jr.	U S I	
do.	I U S	
Miss M. A. Rush,	C U S	
E. N. Cassels,	J P	
J. C. Bell,	35	
B. O. Stout,	B S	
Mrs. E. Paten,	O	
Mrs M. J. Percy,	P	
do.	M P	
J. W. McCampbell,	⊗	
do.	J H B	

GOLIAD COUNTY.

Name	Brand	Earmark
Mrs. Annie Phillips,	A P	
M. S. Coell,	②	
do.	*MG	
Hershell Lacky,	⚥	
B. Owens,	Ⓢ	
Chas. Prescott,	Z5	
do.	J	
T. F. Howell,	EH	
do.	EH	
C. V. Busby,	3 B	
Mrs. R. Ayers,	A R	

GOLIAD COUNTY.

Name	Brand	Mark
Miss M. M. Cossels,	CG	
Stephen Best,	SB	
do.	SB	
Isaac Best,	IB	
H. Best,	HB	
Miss Martha Best,	MƧ	
Miss Georganna Best,	25 on shoulder	
Miss M. L. Best,	53	
A. J. Best,	56	
G. W. Adams.	HE	

GOLIAD COUNTY.

Name	Brand	Mark
W. C. Cartwright,	CW	
Mrs. Jane Stoddard,	SS	
W. S. McCampbell,	S♡	
do.	P	
B. C. Prescott,	2 / 22	
Miss M. J. Sawyer,	MS	
do.	*A	
Mrs. Jane Sawyer,	7I	
do.	DS	
B. F. Middleton,	75	

GOLIAD COUNTY.

G. W. Brumfield,	7C	
do.	OL	
J. W. Kuykendall,	JK	
do.	*3F	
Mrs. H. A. Jackson,	IJ	
J. B. Kuykendall,	J+C	*
do.	73	
do.	37	
Henry Wiltmer,	H⌣	
W. J. McDaniel,	-R	*
Mrs. N. E. Camp,	P	

GOLIAD COUNTY.

M. H. Power,	♀	
Russel Baker,	ᴛR	
Jesse Hassell,	⧖	
W. W. Bruton,	TV	
do.	TVI	
G. W. Winslow,	4J	
G. W. Thompson,	X̄	
Mrs. M. Barfield,	T	
Henry Shaper,	ꓶS	

GOLIAD COUNTY.

293

James Cummings,		
J. G. or J. P. Miller,		
do.	2	
do.	AW	
do.	JJ	
Wm. Evans,	E	
do.	PI	
do.		
do.	3	
do.		

GOLIAD COUNTY.

Mrs. E. Fowler,	Ŧ	⊖⊃⊖⊃
Joseph Stewart,	∫ O	⊂⊃
Miss E. Helper,	ER	⊂⊃
R. Adcock,	∞	⊂⊃
J. H. Sawyer,	5	⊂⊃
Miss A. T. Sawyer,	TS	⊂⊃
do.	*A	
W. H. Gentry,	9	⊖⊃
Wm. Hoff,	JK	
do.	HOF	
do.	*H	

GOLIAD COUNTY.

Robt. Parsons,	H P	
R. Lott or Agt.	LOT	⊂⊃
James Byfield	7Z.	⊂⊃
Elizabeth Furgeson,	7	⊂⊃ * ⊂⊃
Holmes Byfield,	ZL	⊂⊃ * ⊂⊃
M. B. Cassels.	V C	⊂⊃
W. M. Adams,	K	⊂⊃
F. M. Adams,	2S	⊂⊃
Mrs. Mary Dickerson,	A B	⊂⊃ * ⊂⊃
do,	D 3	⊂⊃
do.	J 2	

GOLIAD COUNTY.

Name	Brand	Mark
R. Flowers,	R	
Thomas Gill,	GIL	
Mrs. C. A. Andrews,	.CA	
do.	LA	
Peter Demos,	PD	
do.	TD	
Mrs. E. Brown,	62	
W. W. Rutherford,	E	
W. H. Elkins,	E	
F. Rouse,	R	
Mrs. H. Reynolds,	7	

GOLIAD COUNTY.

Name	Brand	Ear Mark
S. P. Middleton,	P	
Miss M. E. Middleton,	ᴎA	
Mrs. Jane Gray,	8	
do.	*8	
Daniel Blackburn,	D	
Miss C. Hargrave,	ЯR	
C. P. Scott,	(bell)	
do.	(bell)	
do.	⊕	
J. G. Stuart,	S	
do.	*Ⓢ	same ear mark

Mrs. P. Paxton,	P+	⊖⊃⊖⊃
do.	d	
do.	WP	
John P. Reynolds,	ℛ	⊂⊃
S. M. Sessions,	ℐ	⊂⊃
do.	5	⊂⊃
O. Hargrave,	5P	⊖⊃⊂⊃
do.	ℛ	
do.	TT	
do.	ℛ	
W. B. Bridge,	ଌ	⊖⊃

GOLIAD COUNTY.

C M. Jones,	⋈	⊖⊃

MEYERSVILLE P. O.

Adam Skloss,	⍉	⊖⊃
Anton Skloss,	SK	⊖⊃
L. Fromme,	FO	⊖⊃
do.	F	same ear mark
Frederic Dobsky,	D ÿ	⊂⊃
Wm. Meyer,	m	⊖⊃
do.	*FD	⊂⊖
do.	ƆV	⊂⊃
R. Williams,	W 4	⊂⊃

GOLIAD COUNTY.

Henry Jacobs,	HV	
L. Rabbit,	B+	
do.	*LR	
John Urbann,	JU+	
John Arnold,	58	
H. Housman,	HH	
P. A. Jordan,	PJ	
A. Ableski,	AI	
C. Scheffler,	KS	
W. A. Adams,	HO	
Urban Blontzer,	UB	

GOLIAD COUNTY.

Frank Scheffler,

YORKTOWN P. O.

Joseph Ladwyk,

A. Newcomer,

F. G. Newcomer,

Henry Nance,

Henry Hadt,

J. M. Brown,

do.

CONCRETE P. O.

W. C. Riggs,

G. W. Crosson,	2G	
Jacob Fifer,	LF	
N. H. Fifer,	HF	

MISSION VALLEY P. O.

W. H. Davidson,	ED	
do.	52	
do.	AG	
James Maddux,	3S	

NUECES CO. Corpus Christi P. O.

Name	Brand	Mark
Catharine Dunn,	TD	
G. F Evans,	AR	
S. A. Buffum,	S + S	
W. S. K. Mussett,	⌒A	
do.	⌒K	
Mathew Cody,	OK	
John Baskin,	JB	
Patrick Dunn,	S	
George Runnels,	GR	
Peter Curshaw,	R	

NUECES COUNTY.

Tyrey Mussett,	TM	⁓⁓
do.	⌒A	⁓⁓
John Cody,	MK	•⁓•⁓•
Dennis McCoy,	JOD	
do.	JPD	
do.	ER	
do.	OD	
Mathew Cody jr.	IR	⁓⁓
John Dix,	DIX	
John Rabb,	⊻	

Mrs. E. L. Mann.  

Mrs. E. S. Mann,  

Peter Curshaw,  

J. E. Stephens,  

do.  

do.  

H. D. & F. T. Allen,  

do. 

Dennis McCoy,  

do, 

NUECES COUNTY.

A. McLaughlin,	AM	(ear marks)
John Dunn.	JD	(ear marks)
S. W. Fullerton,	STS	
do.	⚓	
Lewis Preston.	LP	(ear marks)

SANDIEGO P. O.

Ramon Cuillar,	(brand)	(ear marks)
Jeronimo Cuillar,	(brand)	(ear marks)
Ramon Garcia,	(brand)	(ear marks)

Francisco Garcia,		
Allahandro Garcia,		
Lucis Garcia,		
Leonisio Mindicta,		
Gens Baldes,		
John Joclin,	JJ	
Dicedena Joclin,	DCJ	
U. Trivenia,	DC	

NUECES COUNTY.

BANQUETE P. O.

M. Fogg,	FM	⊖⊃
R. J. Miller,	M	⊂⊃
do.	Z	
G. W. Cox,	H	⊂⊃
do.	JF	⊂⊃
do.	COX	
B. A. Bennett,	GO	⊖⊃
R. C. Miller,	RP	⊖⊃
W. F. Atkinson,	A	
G. A. & T. L. Rabb,	UI	⊂⊃

NUECES COUNTY.

Purham & Richardson,	P	
J. J. Allsup,	J	⋈
Elizabeth Merrimon,	EM	
James Perkins,	H	
R. C. Ashworth,	Ca	⋈
J. H. Ashworth,	J	⊂⊃
J. J. Ashworth,	B	⋈
J. W. Fogg,	FOG	

NUECES TOWN P. O.

Sena Wright,	XS	⊂⊃

NUECES COUNTY.

Name	Brand	Earmark
Joseph Wright jr,	X̂	
G. F. Wright,	4	
Frank Byler,	⊓	
James B. Gibbs,	Ŀ	
James Gibbs,	C|B	
Rufus Byler,	C2	
T. J. Noakes,	TN	
Harriet Wright	XV	
T. C. Wright,	V	
D. McIntyre,	◇◇	

NUECES COUNTY.

Name	Brand	Mark
D. P. Flint,	⊃⊂	
do.	H	
James Hobbs,	H	
Abraham Byler,	♡	
Wm. Hobbs,	5	

SAN PATRICIO P. O.

Name	Brand	Mark
Francisco Acosta,	Y	
H. C. Wright,	HC	
R. J. Denny,	F	
Samuel Cook,	SC	

NUECES COUNTY.

James McMurry,	JMC	
J. W. Cook,	C	
Eliza Daugherty,	ED	
F. Larema,	A	
F. Belden & Co.	△	
Eustancio Cantu,	A	
Chas. Stillmon jr.	A	

REFUGIO COUNTY. 313

REFUGIO CO. Crescent Village P. O.

Lucas Dubois sr.	S X	⊂⊃
Miss J. Kuykendall,	ƎK	⊂∃ ⊂∃ ⊂∃
Wm. Andrews.	S A	⊂⊃ ⊂⊃
do.	A/	
S. A. Duke,	S	⊂⊃ ⊂⊃
Wm. Kuykendall.	K	⊂∃ ⊂∃
do.	37	
Mrs. E. M. Kuykendall,	M A	⊂∃ ⊂∃ ⊂∃
Lucas Dubois jr.	V Λ	⊂⊃
R. W. McGrew,	10	⊂⊃

REFUGIO COUNTY.

Name	Brand	Earmark
McGrew & Ragland,	CP	
Mrs. A. Givens,	SS	
T. M. Duke jr.	IA	
T. M. Duke sr.	TD	
J. M. Duke,	D	
M. Newsom,	9L	
J. & H. McGrew,	(cup)	
Justilian Dubois,	Jf	
Felix Dubois,	F	
S. L. Townsend,	ST	
do.	ʇ	

Delmar Dubois,	D-D	CD

COPANO P. O.

James Power,	♭	CD
Felipe Power,	FP	CD
Mrs. J. E. Plummer,	JEP	CD

REFUGIO P. O.

W. P. McGrew,	⊖	CD
J. A. Ballard,	HI	CDCD
M. Whelan,	OWEIC3	
do.	OM	

REFUGIO COUNTY.

S. M. Swift,	RS	
W. W. Holbrook,	JP7	⊖⊃
W. W. Holbrook Agt.	DC	⊖⊃
do.	JL	⊖⊃
L. M. Rogers,	R	⊖⊃
Wm. Pierpont,	†P	⊖⊃
do.	*JH	⊖⊃
do.	‡P on left shoulder	C on left hip
John Ryals,	♂	⊖⊃
Mrs. M. Shelly,	SP	⊖⊃⊖⊃
Joseph Jaups,	JF	⊖⊃

REFUGIO COUNTY. 317

J. M. & J. C. Howell,	CN	
do.	♄	
do.	⧖	
H. B. Williams,	HD	⊂⊃
G. J. Brown,	HJ	⊂⊃⊂⊃
do.	*5	⊂⊃
do.	*⋈	⊂⊃
Wm. Reeves.	VR	⊂⊃
do.	2 3	⊂⊃
do.	⧖	⊂⊃
Daniel Fox,	⌶F	⊂⊃

REFUGIO COUNTY.

Mrs. Susan Dugat,	SS	⊖⊕
do.	SIS	⊖⊕
do.	ISI	⊖⊕
do.	⊬S	⊖⊕
do.	J+	⊖⊕
W. Brady or Agt,	⌘	⋈
do.	*H	
do.	*b	
do.	*S3	
do.	*S	
Mrs M. Huddleston,	⅃	⋈
do.	4h	⋈

REFUGIO COUNTY. 319

Garrett Fox,	G	⊂⊃
Robt. Martin,	JR	
J. M. Doughty,	◊	⊂⊃
A. J. West,	⋎	
do.	aR	
do.	Ô	
do.	Æ	
do.	JΓ	
do.	X+	
do.	XG	
do.	JX	

REFUGIO COUNTY.

B. F. West,	ꓞR	brand
B. F. West, Agt.	IR	brand
do.	ꓩ2	brand
do.	R̄D	brand
do.	ⱽR	brand
do.	ꓞɑ	brand
do.	T̄ɑ	brand
do.	ɑR	brand
do.	ꓷR	brand
do.	ϘP	brand
do.	OR	brand

REFUGIO COUNTY. 321

do.	2 Cl	
do.	3 P 1	
do.	3 P 2	
do.	3 P+	
do.	+RC	
do.	7 Cl	
do.	RW	
do.	M	
do.	SD	
do.	J	
do.	Y	

REFUGIO COUNTY.

do.	JE	
do.	55	
do.	J⌐	
do.	⊥Y	
do.	YC	
do.	&V	
do.	RC	
Michael West,	MR	
do.	R	
do.	R	
do.	⊥R	

ST. MARYS P. O.

C. E. Dugat,	MT	(brand marks)
do.	JD	(brand marks)
do.	MD	(brand marks)
do.	CD	(brand marks)
J. R. McCarty,	PP	(ear marks)
T. Welder,	JW	(ear marks)
J. H. Wood,	N	(ear marks)
do.	NC	(ear marks)

REFUGIO COUNTY.

LAMAR P. O.

R. H. Bass,	ᘉᙅ	ᑕᑐ
W. E. Benson,	⟁ (with bar on top)	ᑕᑐ
do.	Ψ	ᑕᑐ
H. Kroeger,	HK	ᑕᑐ (with dots)
Anton Straugh,	℉	ᑕᑐ (with dot)
do.	♡←	

SANPATRICIO CO. Sanpatricio P. O.

John Kellett,	JK	⊖⊃
Wm. Corkill,	(symbol)	
Owen Gaffrey,	OG	⊖⊃
R. B. Hardiman,	JW	
do.	J °¹ jaw	
P. Hart,	PH	⊖⊃
do.	FH	⊖⊃
J. H. Hinrichson,	♡H	⊖⊃
G. F. Jones,	CU	⊖⊃

SAN PATRICIO COUNTY.

Name	Brand	Mark
A. & P. McGloin,	ϚM	
T. McGewin,	VI	
D. W. McWhorter,	⊤P	
S. C. Skidmore,	V	
J. Timon,	JT	
J. H. Toomy,	JT	
J. Waguon,	HV	
J. Whithead,	▽	
J. M. Williamson,	7U	
Martines Lary,	⅄	
Calvin Wright,	53	

ALGUNA P. O.

Name	Brand	Mark
J. Castillo,	ꟼ (G-like)	
J. E. Carroll,	◇C	
R. J. Carroll,	⚓	
Y. Coleman,	⅃L	
J. Polan,	∫	

CORPUS CHRISTI P. O.

Name	Brand	Mark
Mrs. C. A. Burrell,	2 M	
J. E. Coleman,	EC	
B. F. White,	V6	

SAN PATRICIO COUNTY.

| Geo. Allen, | GA⊂⊃⊂⊃ |

VICTORIA CO. Anaqua P. O.

B. Gomes	
J. O. Brien,	oB
R. W. Wellington,	

VICTORIA P. O.

| V. Sattler, | VT |
| Louis Williams, | LV |

MISSION VALLY. P. O.

| Geo. Emison, | Œ |

MASON CO, MASON P. O.

G. W. Todd,	TOD	
do.	*T	
W. C. Lewis,	+	
Lewis & McSween,	Ⓥ	
B. F. Weatherby,	X6	
Conrad Simon.	SI CS	

In future both brands on same animal

J. B. Lindsey,	ML	
do.	JBL	
do.	22	

MASON COUNTY.

Henry Behrens,	61	⊂⊃
John McSween,	?	⊂⊃
do.	℘	⊂⊃
do.	I X	

D. P. Allen,	D	⊂⊃

U. M. Taylor,	DT	⊂⊃
do.	⊙	⊂⊃

GILLESPIE COUNTY.

FREDERICKSBURG P. O.

Name	Brand	Earmark
T. C. Doss'	ID	CD
do.	D	CD
S. A. Dickson,	DI	GD
do.	IOI	GD
Ernest Schafer,	S5	⊃⊂
Ferdinand Dobbler,	FD	ED
C. Brockman,	5	⊃⊂
E. Wahrmund,	EW	⊃⊂
Chas. Feller,	23	ED
C. H. Nimitz,	CN	⊃⊂

GILLESPIE COUNTY.

F. V. D. Stucken,	F	
do.	96	
do,	25	
do.	US	
Joseph White,	W	
Kutscher,	1O	
Kutscher,	O1	
Mathias Shafer,	91	
Ludwig Dobbler,	LD	
John Kallenberg,	K2	
A. Weiss,	62	

GILLESPIE COUNTY.

Jacob Zauner,	ZI	⊂⊃
W. J. Lock,	LOC	⊂⊃
J. H. Lacy,	◇	⊃⊂
L. Harper,	♡	⊃⊂⊃⊂
Milly Doss,	♏P	⊂⊃

KENDALL COUNTY.

KENDALL CO. Boerne P. O.

Name	Brand	Mark
Adam Vogt,	Ψ	
Adam Conrad,	JK	
J. B. Deering,	JB	
J. W. Phillip,	S→	
do.	F	
J. Phillip,	JP	
August Pfeifer		
C. Amann,	AC	
do.	RL	

KENDALL COUNTY.

Name	Brand	Marks
J. M. Patton,	J5	
S. B. Patton,	O	
C. A. Patton,	NP	
James S. Abbott,	H (barred)	
do.	III	*
G. H. Hasckamp,	HH	
Aug. Veigt,	FV	
do.	V	
T. Zoeller.	Z	
F. Vanderstratten,	VC	
do.	ƆƧd	

I. F. Stendebach,		
Anton Koch,		
Gotliebe Stephen,		
do.		
F. Harz,		
do.		
Jacob Sauer,		
T. Vanderstratten,		
F. V. Henderson,		
J. Cummings Evans.		
E. Richter,		

KENDALL COUNTY.

G. W. Kendall,	KB	
do.	⊙	
John Hermann	7·	
Adolph Zoeller,	AZR	
C. Hofäeluz,	Hh	

COMFORT. P. O.

G. Steves,	GS	
R. E. Brown,	ЯB	
do.	SJ	
Mrs. M. E. Harbour,	MH	

F. H. Schlador,	WR	
T. A. Giles,	PS	
do.	P	
T. Weidenfeld,	CW	
H. Seidensticker,	55	
Otto Brinkmann,	OB	
John Hoerner,	HR	
Henry Wittbold,	HW	
Sophia Herbst,	≥ (underlined)	
E. Serger,	LS	

KENDALL COUNTY.

Name	Brand	Earmark
Henry Boerner,	HB	
E. Schilling,	S3	
do.	DS	
M. Lindner,	ML	
F. Saur,	SR	
G. H. Luessmann,	HL	
H. Willie,	W	
do.	JK	
C. Schlader,	CS	
Henry Sauer,	HS	
C. Flach,	CF	

KENDALL COUNTY.

Mrs. E. Allgelt,	⌐┴	⊂⊃
L. Strohecker,	SZ	⊂⊃
C. Haerter,	WH	⊂⊃
Wm. Heuermann,	HD	⊂⊃
Robt. Schaefer,	ℜ	⊂⊃
Aug. Falsin,	AF	⊂⊃
F. Perner,	P	⊂⊃

SISTERDALE P. O.

E. Kapp,	ƎK	⊂⊃

KENDALL COUNTY.

J. Dressel,	Ḋ.	⊖⊋
Christoph Rhodins,	CR	⊂⊃
Mrs. B. Rhodius,	B	⊂⊃

KERR CO. COMFORT P. O.

Name	Brand
E. A. McFadin,	MC
Mrs. E. L. Denton,	F
Joseph M. Denton,	J
L. M. Sennett,	SS
Miss. C. A. Denton,	C
Miss Amanda Sennett	A
H. Ingenhuett,	VE
F. Dietert jr.	Di
E. Schwethelm,	⚱

KERR COUNTY. 343

G. Schellhase,	⌁	
F. Schulze,	F₂	
Rudolph Voigt,	RV	
H. Allerkamp,	HA	
Robert Steves,	RS	
W. C. Boerner,	←G	
O. Roggenbucke,	OR	
G. Stieler,	St	
C. Karger,	15	
Chas. Heinen,	17	

KERR COUNTY.

KERRVILLE P. O.

H. M. Burney,	H	⊖⊃
W. A. Lowrence,	+	⊂⊖*⊂⊖
D. B. Lowrence,	+L	

ZANZENBURG P. O.

M. M. Connor,	CO⊖⊃*⊂⊃	
J. A. Connor,	JO	⊖⊃

GONZALES CO. Gonzales P. O.

R. H. Floyd,	20	CE ED
do.	*R̂	CE ED
do.	*JF	EƎ EƎ
C. Lemond,	SL	C•Ɔ C•Ɔ
J. H. Wilson,	JB	CƆ
W. Duren,	H	C•Ɔ CƐƆ CƆ
S. N. Hall,	SH	CƐ
J. W. J. Alldridge,	A	EƎ EƎ
Benj. Power,	BP	EƆ EƆ

GONZALES COUNTY.

E. C. Frisbie,	F 5	
Mrs. L. Arrington.	LN	
J. T. Price,	J P	
A. J. Nations,	NO	
W. M. Pierson,	MP	
E. Womack,	E I	
C. B. Child,	BC	
R. J. Gill,	R C	
do.	①	
Baker & Fulcher,	D D	

GONZALES COUNTY.

J. R. Gipson,	♃	⊂⊃
Mrs. S. E. Davis,	DA	⊂⊃
H. H. Mills,	T I	⊂⊃
W. T. B. Wells.	T 6	⊂⊃
B. E. Anderson,	WA	⊂⊃
John Putman,	I I 2	⊂⊃
S. V. Putman,	V P	⊂⊃
A. C. Smith,	X I	⊂⊃
do.	*I X	
do.	*∧S	
do.	*S ♡	⊂⊃

348 GONZALES COUNTY.

Name	Brand	Mark
W. A. Ritchie,	CR	
Wm. Billings,	WK	
A. Lambert,	O	
Thomas Lambert,	↑	
do.	*BO	
J. A. & W. L. Barnett,	◇	
Eliza Barnett,	33	
L. P. Bundick	40	
M. P. Bundick	Pb	
H. Riley	UR	
M. T. Loyd	YI	

GONZALES COUNTY.

Name	Brand	Mark
R. Newsom,	R N	
A. B. Johnson,	X V	
W. M. Hancock,	E E	
N. Mitchell.	N 3	
Morris May,	Ⓜ	
J. N. Dulaney,	D O C	
Robt. A. Atkinson,	R A	
Henry Caraway jr.	S L	
D. B. Dillard,	D L	
Joseph O Conner,	O C	

23

S. B. Conley.	8T	
Henry Caraway sr.	JH	⊂∞
do.	H	
W. Oneill,	VL	⊂⊃
J. J. Caraway,	⊣₁	⊂⊃
do.	L2	⊂⊃
do.	A	⊂⊃
B. A. Passmore,	7P	⊂⊃
Mrs. M. A. Vandegrift,	VAN	⊂⊃
do.	VC	
do.	.7V	

GONZALES COUNTY. 351

G. W. Henry,	JL	
K. S. Caraway, jr.	TI	
Henry Carpenter,	7A	
W. L. Caraway,	8P	
K. S. Caraway, sen.	T	
Mrs. C. Miller,	CM	
M. Trafton,	Un	
do.	TL	
do.	UT	
J. F. Beasley,	JF	
do.	2M	

GONZALES COUNTY.

J. F. Martin,	C2	
do.	C4	
do.	-C2	
Mrs. L. Carpenter,	WC	
do.	*C	
G. Billings,		
W. C. Billings,	JH	
Wm. Putman,	WP	
H. C. Wright,	JJ	
A. Avant,	4O	
Wm. Putman jr.	P	

GONZALES COUNTY.

Name	Brand	Earmark
Mrs. Fannie Benham,	F̂	
do.	*P̂	
S. B. Lambert,	F	
F. M. Clary	gy	
John Mill,	ÔS	
L. C. Wright,	DW	
do.	H1	
do	cv	
J. W. Davis,	—C	
J. T. Mathien,	(L)	
Mrs. E. Morrow,	7	

354 GONZALES COUNTY.

Name	Brand	Mark
N. J. Hoover,	∫H	
J. N. Rogers,	TѲ	
G. D. Mitchell,	q q	
J W. Lemmond.	JL	
do.	⌐ on hip J on jaw	
W. S. McAda,	HE	
G. P. Darden,	ԸD	
Mrs. Nancy Baker,	ꓭ	
T. N. Mathews,	T◇	
do.	Q	
J. W. Dikes,	ᶇD	

GONZALES COUNTY.

Name	Brand	Mark
W. L. Dubose,	D	
Jasper Billings,	?	
Mrs Nancy Burton,	I I	
R. H. Carson,	C4	
James Nations,	N	
Jas. & Robt. Nations	NA	
do,	*NA	
J. T. Nations,	JN	
Miss M. F. Wilkinson,	M4	
F. Chenault,	U	

GONZALES COUNTY

Name	Brand	Ear marks
Mrs Emma King,	OO	
do.	O	
L. Nichols	Nic	
J. M. Lookingbill,	JML	
W. T. Brown,	TWB	
James Anderson,	⌐	
J. M. Canterbury,	♦♥	
Samuel Pease,	SP	
M. G. S. Coulter,	④	
do.	2M	

GONZALES COUNTY. 357

T. F. Rancy,	TR	CS
John Bratton,	☽	⋈
do.	☽ horse brand on jaw	J On back part of thigh.
L. M. Rayborn,	♡ (with arrow)	
Clemens & Rayborn,	4	

RANCHO P. O.

J. G. Morey & Bros.	5 1	
do.	*⊖	
do.	* V 5	
do.	* V 2	
do.	* V5	

do.	* VL
do.	* V2
do.	* N̲
do.	* N̲̄
do.	* VL
do.	* N
do.	* 5 I
	* COL
do.	* ⊖
do.	* ⌣ Old stock contra-branded with ᗡ̌ or ᗡ
do.	N̄
do.	5 I ☾☽

GONZALES COUNTY.

do.	COL	
do.	OIO	
do.	*RAK	
do.	*JO	
do.	*RA	
Wm. Bundick,	2b	
do.	V3	
Martin Bundick,	3S	
Jonathan Scott,	8	
N. H. Scott,	S	
do.	S	

GONZALES COUNTY.

Mrs. E. Gillespie,	GGI	
do.	GG	
Mrs. M. Gillespie,	GG	
do.	JG	
J. C. Gillespie,	JIM	
do.	JG	
James M Murray,	PU	
Mrs M E Murray,	J	
do.	EY	
do.	⌒	
do.	♡	

Name	Brand	Mark
J. R. Murray,	IVI	
Mrs. M. Callison,	SC	
J. C. Callison,	J2	
John McPeters,	♡	
Thomas McPeters,	♡	
Geo. McPeters,	GM	
W. K. Estill,		
John Sikes,	A	
C. White,		
do.		
H. J. Weber,		

GONZALES COUNTY.

Name	Brand	Mark
F. M. Marcum,	(symbol)	
do.	X5	
do.	(symbol)	
Roswell Gillett,	RG	
Chas. Forester,	2X	
Mrs R. Davis,	ZD	
Mrs. E. Forester,	ZF	
W. Bartlett,	D	
Mrs M. Sikes,	RM	
E. T. Pierson,	MV	
J. G Fanning,	JGF	

GONZALES COUNTY.

Name	Brand	Mark
C J Hanson,	IM	(ear marks)
B B Gillett.	FF	
J M Maugum,	72	(ear marks)
Miss E T Maugum,	EM	(ear marks)
L L Maugum,	JI	(ear marks)
A C Reves,	H	(ear marks)
H F Hall,	H̄	(ear marks)
J M Sullevant,	UV	(ear marks)
S H Nowlin,	⑤	(ear marks)
J W Dickey,	JE	(ear marks)
Mrs P J Dickey,	DU	(ear marks)

Name	Brand	Mark
S. Wiley,	U̲P̲	
W M Gay,	SP	

BELMONT P. O.

Name	Brand	Mark
Joseph McCoy,	J	
Alfred Morris,	3M	
Miss E Williams,	EL	
N M Smiley.	SN	
J T Tally,	UT	
W H Burris,	24	
do.	X	

GONZALES COUNTY.

Mrs. M. Burrows,	M5	
do.	ZI	
W. F. M. Holms,	HL	
E. Y. Seale,	B	
J. J. Foster,	F	
E. R. Hurt,	Y	
W. B. McGuffin,	A2	
G. W. Lookingbill,	GL	
W. F. Harper,	WH	
M. T. Little,		

E. F. Morris,	2F	
G. W. Pierce,	CP	
C. McCoy,	MC	
Mrs. C. McCoy,	♡2	
Mrs. S. Clark,	C	
H. O'Neal,	V5	
do.	V2	
B. Collins,	A	
P. C. McCoy,	M	
P. B. Littlefield,	PL	

GONZALES COUNTY.

Name	Brand	Mark
J. W. Burris,	O7	
do.	7	
N. W. Guinn.	NG	
Mrs. S. H. Moore	E	
S. A. Hubbard,	⌿E	
J. A. Swan,	◇◇	
L. S. McCoy,	2L	
Texas McCoy,	U	
Mrs. S. McCoy,	⌿J	*
D. F. Webb,	F	

GONZALES COUNTY.

W. C. Barnes,	HB	C3
James T. Foster,	F	C3
J. W. Foster,	cF	
P. Dilworth,	◇T◇	C3
A. M. Robbins,	A2	C3
D. P. Briggs,	P5	C3
L. N. West,	LW	C3

CONCRETE P. O.

James Monroe.	MO	
do.	*F	
Mrs. Jane Harper,	∧3	
M. M. Elder,	ME	
R. H. Hester.	RH	
G. W. Davis,	WD	
do.	K	
S. S. Pearson,	M	
do.	MP	
L. A. Preston,	♡♡	

ROUND LAKE P. O.

S. P. Bundick,	F6	(brand)
Mrs. M Weber,	人	(brand)
Mrs. M. B. Clements,	S♡	(brand)
do.	♡	
C. Clements,	⊓ / T	(brand)
do.	↑	

YORKTOWN P. O.

John Billings,	JB	(brand)
Mrs. Harriet Hesson,	人	(brand)

GONZALES COUNTY. 371

Name	Brand	Mark
L. Quinney,	6	
Mrs. R. Quinney,	?	
Fred Duderstadt,	L1	
Miss J. Duderstadt,	L2	
Andres Duderstadt,	LD	
John Duderstadt,	TU	
S. E Sommerville,	SS	
J. W. S. Christman,	SS	
William Pierson,	MP	
Miss Louisa Asher,	T♥	

GONZALES COUNTY.

Franklin Freeman,

do.

F. Asher,

Thomas Caffal,

J. B. Hand.

COUNTY INDEX.

Atascosa..........117	Karnes............58
Bandara............20	Kendall..........334
Bee................93	Kerr.............342
Bexar............182	Live Oak.........301
Comal............147	Medina............25
Dawson............69	McMullen.........177
Dimmitt..........146	Mason............329
DeWitt...........250	Nueces...........383
Frio.............142	Refugio..........313
Guadeloupe.......234	Sanpatricio......523
Goliad...........284	Uvalde.............5
Gillespie........331	Victoria.........328
Gonzales.........345	Wilson............83

ALPHABETICAL INDEX.

NAMES.	PAGES.	NAMES.	PAGES
Adams, W. C.	3	Avent, A. J.	216
Adams, P. T. & M. V.	5	Avent, F. M.	216
Adams, D. G.	6	Adams, J. M.	218
Adams, J. M.	6	Ackermann, A. A.	218
Anglen, Aaron	12	Adams & Lytle,	219
Allen, Warren	12	Aue, Max.	228
Allen, Mrs. Paulina	19	Altweih, Gustave	236
Allen, Miss Virginia	19	Acker, Mrs. M. J.	238
Adamietz, Albert	20	Asher, Mrs. Catharine	239
Allen, A.	40	Amacher, M.	241
Aden, E.	46	Anderson, John R.	246
Allof, Henry	55	Applewhite, Mrs. Elizabeth	248
Austin, A.	59	Anderson, Walter	252
Ammons, H. R.	65	Anderson, Richmond	252
Archie, Mrs. R.	72	Afflerbach, J.	252
Asher, James	83	Aaron, Wm.	254
Arcenega, G.	87	Afflerbach, H.	258
Aguilar, Nepumuseno	88	Anderson, Wyatt	258
Anya, Ysable	93	Ainsworth, J. P.	260
Alderte, Jesus	93	Allee, Alfred	269
Avala, Jose M.	94	Ashworth, Moses or agt.	278
Alisup, B. M. G. or agt.	102	Ayers, Mrs. R.	288
Allsup, T. M. & R. A.	102	Adams, G. W.	289
Allsup, Mrs. N. C.	102	Adcock, R.	294
Atkins, John	106	Adams, W. M.	295
Althouse, J. H.	108	Adams, F. M.	295
Areola, Louis	119	Andrews, Mrs. C. A.	296
Arnold, Daniel	119	Arnold, John	300
Areola, Refugio	123	Ableski, A.	300
Areola, Mrs. Guadalupe	124	Adams, W. A.	900
Aikmann, Miss Caroline	124	Allen, H. D. & F. T.	305
Allen, A.	133	Atkinson, W. F.	308
Appman, Geo.	153	Allsup, J. J.	309
Artz, Gustive	154	Ashworth, R. C.	309
Artz, Gotliebe	159	Ashworth, J. J.	309
Akermann, Charles	162	Ashworth, J. H.	309
Adams, J. Q.	182	Acosta, Francisco	311
Adams, Mrs. Sarah	192	Andrews, Wm.	313
Anderson, Joseph	183	Allen, Geo.	328
Areola, Antonio	194	Allen, D. P.	330
Alameda, Jose	196	Amann C.	334
Applewhite, Jesse	210	Abbott, James S.	335

INDEX.

NAMES.	PAGES.	NAMES.	PAGES.
Altgelt, Mrs. E.	340	Atkinson, Robt. A.	349
Allerkamp, H.	343	Avant, A.	352
Alldridge, W. J.	345	Anderson, James.	356
Arrington, Mrs. L.	346	Asher, Miss Louisa	371
Andersen, B. E.	347	Asher, F.	372
Bates, E. A.	6	Bomfalk, Harm	52
Boon, J. L. C.	6	Balzan, H. H.	52
Brown, G. W.	6	Britz, Peter	56
Bowls, W. B.	10	Bolt, Martin	57
Brown, J. G.	11	Binnion, John	57
Brown, W. A.	12	Bolt, Chas.	58
Bowls, Greenville	13	Butler, A. B.	63
Bandy, James J.	20	Butler, James B.	63
Bandy, Thomas	20	Barfield, J. H.	63
Bird, B. F.	21	Borroum, J. B.	64
Bird, Miss Armenia	21	Baylor, J. W.	64
Bird, Charles	21	Barfield, C. J.	65
Benseman, H.	23	Butler, Burnell	67
Becker, J.	25	Brown, G. W.	69
Bendele, Joseph	25	Barfield, I. C.	71
Burrell, Joseph	26	Bowen, Neel	71
Becker, T. C. G.	27	Biela, Frank	73
Becker, Mathias	27	Brondar, Caspar	73
Boyls, Mrs. Lydia P.	28	Bishop & Johnson	73
Bader, Joseph sen.	30	Beverly, H. M.	73
Bader, Sebastian	31	Banduch, Paul	74
Boon, S.	31	Brysh, Michael	74
Bader, Mary	31	Bronder, Simon	75
Bader, Joseph jr.	31	Burda, Frank	78
Billharz, Joseph	34	Bonk, Anton	79
Bendele, Andres	37	Boon, James	79
Brown, Edward	37	Belding, W. G.	80
Brown, Mrs. D.	37	Brown, Solomon	82
Beck, Benhard	38	Burt, Wm.	82
Bendele, Jacob	38	Birdsall, Lockwood	83
Burrell, John B.	40	Butler, J. C.	84
Blackaller, James	41	Barclay, C. M.	85
Bloss, Adam	42	Baylor, W. K.	85
Burrows, W. A.	43	Barnes, James	90
Burrows, John B.	43	Barker, S. W.	91
Burnett, Tally	44	Bueno, Juan	93
Bailey, Mrs. E.	47	Bala, Juan	96
Balzan, Harm	47	Bigner, J. A.	100
Borchers, Henry	47	Brown, James	104
Bender, Mrs. Caterina	48	Bradley, Miss M. J. & sisters	105
Boehle, Louis	49	Burk, Patrick	107
Bailey, Wilson	49	Barber, Benj.	115
Brooks, Henry	51	Bradley, Chas.	116
Britsch, Gottlieb	51	Barksdale, J. O. C.	117

INDEX.

NAMES.	PAGES.	NAMES.	PAGES.
Barksdale, W. J.	117	Beeze, J.	185
Barksdale, L., Est. of	118	Bennett, D. W.	191
Barksdale, Mrs. M. or ag't,	118	Bargas, Agapo	196
Bell, J. W.	121	Brandy, Francis	200
Bell, M. D.	122	Bucharti, E.	200
Blevins, Andrew J.	123	Beitle, Joseph	204
Barksdale, W. P.	125	Beitle, F. J.	204
Barksdale, L. F.	125	Beitle, C. F.	204
Beall, P. C.	128	Belvin, R. H.	207
Brite, Thos. Est. of	128	Bright, James M.	210
Barnes, Mrs. M. J.	131	Buechsenschnetz, G. H.	212
Brite, John H.	135	Briggs, E.	213
Bennett, H.	142	Bacon, J. C.	213
Bennett, Mrs. M.	142	Bacon, E. B.	214
Bennett, A. C.	142	Bering, Aug.	215
Bennett, Cloid	142	Barker, S. J.	216
Bennett, Daniel	142	Barker, G. A.	216
Burleson, Ed	142	Burrell, J. B.	222
Burleson, Henry	143	Burrell, Jacob	222
Burleson, Jacob & H.	143	Boehme, F. A.	222
Berry, Mrs. Carolina	144	Becker, Martin,	222
Berry, Miss M.	144	Brown, J. H.	223
Berry, Miss Ann E.	144	Byer, Anton	228
Berry, John	145	Brown, J. B.	230
Burleson, John,	145	Brahan, R. W.	232
Bell, Leonard L,	146	Baker, Fredk.	234
Brecher, Jacob	147	Bauer, Angust	235
Bracht, Felix	149	Blumberg, T. A.	237
Bremer, Miss Annie	153	Bartels, Wm.	237
Bremer, Miss E. & A.	153	Reiler, Christopher,	242
Busch, Christian	154	Barruss, J. H.	243
Bitter, Henry	154	Brotze, Mrs. D.	243
Bueche, A. L.	157	Brotze, C.	243
Burckardt, G.	157	Brotze, Otto,	243
Barbe, Heinrich	158	Bergfeld, J. G.	244
Bielstien, Mrs. C.	158	Brooks, John,	245
Busch, Henry	159	Brown, Sanford,	245
Bairle, Sebastian	161	Barker, E. A.	249
Butler, W. T. C.	163	Barker, E. C.	249
Bartlett, J. B.	164	Brown, S.	252
Bell, Sebastian	164	Boldt, Fredk.	258
Brouan P. C.	167	Boldt, Lebrecht,	259
Bymum & Ferrell	167	Buer, Fredk.	256
Butler, Albert,	166	Braunig, Mrs. C.	262
Bell, Samuel	171	Basley, T. J.	265
Brown, R. A,	177	Brantly, J. D.	265
Brown, C. W.	177	Borchers, I. H.	267
Brown, Mrs. S. A.	177	Bennett, O. H.	267
Brown, W. J.	177	Bay, John M.	269
Brown, M. C.	177	Blackwell, W. A.	269
Bowen, John	185	Bell, J. M.	270

INDEX.

NAMES.	PAGES.	NAMES.	PAGES.
Brown, Fred.	279	Byler, Abraham,	311
Brooks, G. W. jr.	272	Belden, F. & Co.	312
Brooks, J. M.	272	Ballard, J. A.	315
Brooks, G. W., sen.	272	Brown, G. J.	317
Boston, H B.	273	Brady, W., or agent	318
Brown, Robt.	273	Bass, R. H.	324
Blackwell, M.	276	Benson, W. E.	324
Benking, A. F.	277	Burrell, Mrs. C. A.	327
Brown, Mrs. Mary	277	Brien, J. O.	328
Brown, Miss D. E.	278	Behrens, Henry	330
Brown, W, C. & C. F.	278	Brockman, C.	331
Bitterly, Joseph,	280	Brown, R. E.	337
Burk, E. N.	281	Bunkmann, Otto	338
Bichrig, Andres	282	Boerner, Henry	339
Bell, Mrs. M. A.	284	Boerner, W. C.	243
Bowen, Green	884	Boggenbuke, O.	343
Bell, J. C.	287	Burney H. M.	344
Busby, C. V.	288	Billings, Wm.	348
Best, Stephen,	289	Barnett, J. A. & W. L.	348
Best; Isaac,	289	Barnett, Eliza	388
Best, H.	289	Bundick, L. P.	348
Best, Miss Martha	289	Bundick, M. P.	348
Best, Miss Georgiana	289	Beasley, J. F.	351
Best, Miss M. L.	289	Billings, G.	352
Best, A. J.	289	Billings, W. C.	352
Brumfield, G. W.	291	Benham, Mrs. Fannie	353
Baker, Russel,	292	Baker, Mrs. Nancy	354
Bruton, W. W.	292	Billings, Jasper	355
Barfield, Mrs. M.	292	Burton, Mrs. Nancy	355
Byfield, James	295	Brown, W. T.	356
Byfield, Holmes	295	Bratton, John	357
Brown, Mrs. E.	296	Bundick, Wm.	359
Blackburn, Dan'l	297	Bundick, Martin	359
Bridge, W. B.	298	Bartlett, W.	362
Blontzer, Urban,	300	Burris, W. H.	364
Brown, J. M.	301	Burrows, Mrs. M.	365
Buffum, S. A.	303	Burris, J. W.	367
Buskin, John	303	Barnes, W. C.	368
Baldes, Gens	307	Briggs, D. P.	368
Bennett, B. A.	308	Bundick, S. P.	370
Byler Frank	310	Billings, John	370
Byler, Rufus	310		
Cook, David	6	Crane, W. A.	12
Cook, W. T.	6	Cantwell, Sam'l.	19
Crawford, John C.	7	Chipman, Miss M. M.	20
Cummings, J. W.	8	Clark Amasa	21
Crane, J. H.	12	Chipman, E. A.	21

INDEX.

NAMES.	PAGES.	NAMES.	PAGES.
Conrad, Joseph	30	Corrigan, Mrs. Ellen	107
Courand, Jos.	35	Carroll, Michael	107
Christillis, George	36	Carroll, Wm.	107
Christillis, Mrs. M. S.	36	Carroll, John	107
Christilis, Jos.	36	Clare, H. T.	111
Chassard, Peter	36	Clare, John I.	111
Conrad Peter,	40	Clare, J. F., Est. of	111
Cosgrove, John;	57	Campbell, Mrs. S.	115
Chambers, Mrs. M.	57	Carver, Isaac	124
Chesner, Mrs. Nancy,	59	Camp, John	125
Caloway, W. R.	60	Carr & Johnson	131
Case, Gordon	62	Cavender, Mrs. S. A.	134
Chandler, Thomas,	62	Cavender, J. F.	134
Clark H. J.	62	Cavender, Miss F. E.	134
Crain, Taylor	63	Curry, R. A.	136
Crain, G. W.	63	Crawford, Jas. M.	136
Crain, John D.	63	Caruthers, Wm.	138
Cocke, J. R.	63	Cooper, J. W. & I. N.	139
Cocke V. F.	64	Cowan, I. M.	139
Cooper, George	64	Cruz, Juan Jose de la	139
Coltrain, Morgan	64	Cruz, Juan de la	139
Cocke, F. B. S., sen.	64	Cruz, Gasper de la	139
Cooper, J. D.	65	Cruz, Rafola de la	140
Carmichael, J. S.	66	Cruz, Lauro de la	140
Cook, L. D.	68	Calhoun, J.	152
Cook & Wright,	69	Conring, F. L. H.	153
Cocke, F. B, S., jun.	69	Carson, John	160
Campbell, J. W.	71	Coker, Alex.	163
Czerner, Albert	74	Chambles, H. F.	170
Collingsworth, G. M.	76	Chambles, John	170
Coy, Trinidad	76	Chambles, M. C.	171
Coy, Mrs. T.	77	Crow, Edwin D.	171
Caspzick, Joseph	77	Cox, C. C.	172
Cochran, W. M.	80	Clark, Wm.	175
Campbell Collin	81	Crain, W. P.	178
Cantu, Vicente	86	Coker, J. H.	183
Cantu, Juan	86	Cotton, W. D.	183
Castaneda, T.	87	Casnova, Simon	189
Carmona, Cesario	88	Casnova, R,	189
Cantu, Agapeto	90	Coker, Sampson	190
Castillo, Mrs. Juana	92	Coopwood, Bethel	190
Cruz, Bonito	92	Capps, Ransom	190
Curvier, Matias	93	Coker, Joseph	191
Cruz, Nicholas	94	Carillo, Martias	195
Cline & Helduson	94	Carillo, Isabel	195
Curvier, Juan	96	Castillo, Maria de Jesus	195
Cone, Walker & Co.	98	Castillo, Dario	195
Carter, Giles	105	Casillas, Casimero	196
		Casillas, Marcelo	196

NAMES.	PAGES.	NAMES.	PAGES.
Cashell, A. L.	199	Cox, G. W.	308
Childers, M. M.	201	Cook, Sam'l	311
Campbell, R. B.	205	Cook, J. W.	312
Campbell, L.	205	Cantu, Eustancio	312
Cloud, J. R.	207	Corkill, Wm.	325
Childress, Sol. C.	208	Castillo, J.	327
Childress, Polk & Sam.	208	Carroll, J. E.	327
Corry, T. F.	208	Carroll, R. J.	327
Cass, Josiah	216	Coleman, Y.	327
Crownover, Arthur	220	Coleman, J. E.	327
Clark, Owen	220	Conrad, Adam	334
Cagnion, A. & E.	221	Conner, M. M.	344
Clark, G. W.	228	Conner, J. A.	344
Cunningham, Est. of T.	232	Child, C. B.	346
Conrad, Carl	244	Caraway, Henry, jun.	349
Campbell, Mrs. Martha	247	Conly, S. B.	350
Camdbell, John	347	Caraway, Henry, sen.	350
Conch, Wm. E.	250	Caraway, K. S., sen.	351
Carni, August	264	Caraway, J. J.	350
Cox, J. B.	270	Caraway, K. S., jun.	351
Caruthers, Mrs. Cyrena	270	Carpenter, Henry	351
Calhoun, S. D.	270	Caraway, W. L.	351
Christian, Robt.	285	Carpenter, Mrs. L.	352
Cassels, E. N.	287	Clary, F. M.	353
Coell, M. S.	288	Carson, R. H.	355
Cassels, Miss M. M.	289	Chenault, F.	355
Cartwright, W. C.	290	Canterberry, J. M.	356
Camp, Mrs. N. E.	291	Coulter, M. G. S.	356
Cummings, Jas.	293	Clemons & Rayborn	357
Cassels, M. B.	295	Callison, Mrs. M.	361
Crosson, G. W.	302	Callison, J. C.	361
Cody, Mathew	303	Clark, Mrs. S.	366
Curshaw, Peter	303	Collins, B.	366
Cody, John	304	Clements, Mrs. M. B.	370
Cody, Mathew, jun.	304	Clements, C.	370
Curshaw, Peter	305	Christman, J. W. S.	371
Cuillar, Ramon	306	Caffal, Thomas	372
Cuillar, Jeronimo	306		
Davis, Dan	7	Deras, John	32
Dale, E. V.	8	Deras, Mrs. Catherine	35
Daugherty, J. Q.	10	Dean, Mrs. E. L.	45
Davenport, John	12	Decker, Joseph	47
Davenport, Mrs. Mary	13	Denis, John H.	48
Davenport, L. C.	13	Davis, N.	53
Davenport, A. J.	13	Downs, E. M.	53
Dillard, A. B.	13	Dorn, Rob't	55
Dillard, Allen	13	Davis, Miss Florence	58
Dillard, Joseph	13	Davis, Isham	61
Davenport, J. B.	17	Drake, Orin	62

INDEX. 379

NAMES.	PAGES.	NAMES.	PAGES.
Darden, J. E.	70	Davenport, Wm.	230
Dzink, John	75	Day, Thos.	236
Dugi, Albert	75	Dietz, Ferdinand	244
Dietzman, Stephen	77	Dugger, H. A.	244
Dworatzek, Jakob	77	Duerr, Wm.	255
Dromgoole, Mrs. T.	80	Dahlman, Chas.	260
Dees, J. B.	82	Denson, J. M.	264
Delgado, Juan	92	Delony, L. H.	269
Delgado, Refugio	92	Dow, Jas. M.	269
Duian, Antonio	93	Drier, Gideon	278
Delgado, Jose M.	95	Diebel, Christoph	280
Dodd, Mrs. J. E.	100	Duderstadt, F.	281
Dykes, J. P.	107	Dickerson, Mrs. Mary	295
Dossey, Miss M. C.	120	Demos, Peter	296
Dossey, G. W.	120	Dobsky, Fredk	299
Dossey, W. G.	120	Davidson, W. H.	302
Dickens, Thos. E.	132	Dunn, Catharine	303
Dial, James jr.	137	Dunn, Patrick	303
Duck, G. W. M.	138	Dix, John	304
Daugherty, H. M.	143	Dunn, John	306
Dickens, Wm.	146	Denny, R. J.	311
Diesselhorst, Th.	153	Daugherty, Eliza	312
Dietz, Miss M.	161	Dubois, Lucas sr.	313
Dodson, A. B.	165	Duke, S. A.	313
Dodson, M. M.	167	Dubois, Lucas jr.	313
Dalton, J. H.	171	Duke, T. M. sr.	314
Drury, J. W. or agt.	171	Duke, T. M. jr.	314
Dolan, James	173	Duke, J. M.	314
Daugherty, Robert	173	Dubois, Justillian	314
Dolan, M.	174	Dubois, Felix	314
Dolan, Mrs. E.	174	Dubois, Delmar	315
Dolan, Thos.	174	Dugat, Mrs. Susan	318
Dolan, John	174	Doughty, J. M.	319
Dix, O. T.	181	Dugat, C. E.	323
Devine, Daniel	182	Doss, T. C.	331
Dunn, James Est. of	182	Dickson, S. A.	331
Dewey, E. C.	185	Dobbler, Ferdinand	331
Dauchey, A. N.	186	Dobbler, Ludwig	332
Desmuke, A. W.	188	Doss, Milly	333
Dwyer, Mrs. E.	193	Deering, J. B.	334
Diaz, Margarita	194	Dressel, J.	341
Diaz, Guadaloupe	194	Denton, Mrs. E. S.	342
Diaz, Juana F.	197	Denton, Joseph M.	342
Dashiel, T. P.	202	Denton, Miss C. A.	342
DeVilbiss, J. W.	204	Dietert, F. Jr.	342
Durler, J. J.	208	Duren, W.	345
Dillon, Arthur	219	Davis, Mrs. S. E.	347
Drown, Mrs. E. A.	219	Dulany, J. N.	349
Dobbin, John	220	Dillard, D. B.	349
Droitcourt, Jacob	225	Davis, J. W.	353

INDEX.

NAMES.	PAGES.	NAMES.	PAGES.
Darden, G. P.	354	Dilworth, P.	368
Dikes, J. W.	354	Davis, G. W.	369
Dubose, W. L.	355	Duderstadt, Fred	371
Davis, Mrs. R.	362	Duderstadt, Miss J.	371
Dickey, J. W.	363	Duderstadt, Andres	371
Dickey, Mrs. P. J.	363	Duderstadt, John	371
Evans, W. M.	10	Evans, R. B.	232
Eit, A.	47	Ewel, J. B.	233
Eckhart, Christian	50	Ebert, Aug.	235
Elam, Jeff.	56	Eberling, Fred.	236
Elam, John	56	Engelke, Conrad	236
Eckford, N. W.	59	Ernst, Fred.	237
Elder, J. M.	67	Elly, C. R.	239
Evans, N. B.	69	Elam, Wm. R.	242
Estrado, Francisco	96	Eahl, Fred.	244
Esparza, Auricas	120	Evans, heirs	246
Esparza, Manuel	123	Edwards, E. M	254
Evans, John E.	133	Eckhardt, Caeser	256
English, Mrs. M.	142	Eckhardt, Robt. C.	257
English Jonathan	142	Eckhardt, Wm.	257
English, Mrs. Margaret,	142	Eckhardt, Herman	257
Eastwood, Leonard	143	Engels, Bernard	259
Eastwood James	143	Escalaro, Joseph	267
Engleman, Martin,	150	Epperson, Mrs. Sarah	271
Esser, Charles	162	Eckhardt, Ben	282
Edes, M. V,	166	Evans, Wm.	293
Ellis, John	169	Elkins, W. H.	296
Evans, Mrs. Margaret	175	Evans, G. F.	303
Ellermann, Henry	186	Emison, Geo.	328
Edwards, C. G.	187	Evans, J. Cummings	336
Espinosa, Pedro	194	Estill, W. K.	361
Epp, John	219	Elder, M. M.	369
Fleming, O. D.	14	Flores, N.	90
Fleming, L.	14	Flores, Mrs. M. L. S. de	90
Fenly, Joel D.	14	Flores, Yssidro	92
Fenly, John M.	14	Flores, Pedro	93
Fenly Joel C.	14	Flores, Jose	94
Fenly, C. D.	14	Falcon, Beanino	95
Fenly, James M.	14	Fuller, E. T.	99
Flores, Andres	19	Fadden, John	100
Faseler, G. H.	49	Fuller, T. estate of	104
Ford, H. D.	65	Fisher, Mrs. W.	104
Flippin, Mr a Sarah	66	Fox, J. H.	104
Ford, B.	81	Fitzgerald, A. or agt.	105
Flores, Miss Librado	87	Foster, J. M.	106
Flores, Juan F.	89	Fellers, M. G.	108

INDEX.

NAMES.	PAGES	NAMES.	PAGES
Fox, M., Est. of	110	Ferris, Morris	240
Fuller, Mrs. C., or agent	114	Faris, J. W.	250
Fadden, Patrick	115	Friar, Jack Hays	250
Fox, Andrew	116	Fleming, M.	251
Fountain, H. C.	117	Fleming, Miss M. J.	251
Fuller, B. F.	120	Fort, Mrs. Harriet A.	251
Fuller, James H.	120	Faris, Dan'l	260
Fest, Miss Rosina	124	Faris, T. J.	260
Foster, T. R.	124	Faris, Jas. W.	262
French, Marcellus	126	Fleming, Mrs. Si F.	265
Fields, E.	128	Frazier, J. N.	267
Fuller, John S.	130	Faber, H.	275
Frame, Wm., Est. of	135	Fuchs, Nicholas	273
Frame, Mrs. M., or agent	135	Fuchs, Otto	282
Franks, B. F., Eest. of	144	Fowler, Mrs. E.	294
Franks, J. B.	144	Furgeson, Mrs. Eliz.	295
Forster, Friedrick	147	Flowers, R.	296
Faigaux, F. H.	148	Fromme, L.	299
Fischer, Charles	148	Fifer, Jacob	302
Forester, Edward	152	Fifer, N. H.	302
Fei, Valentine	157	Fullerton, S. W.	306
Fuhrmann, Valentine	162	Fogg, M.	308
Frazer, G. W.	167	Fogg, J. W.	309
Ferrell, B. C.	167	Flint, D. P.	311
Ferrell, Mrs. M.	168	Fox, Dan'l	317
Francis, John R.	173	Fox, Garrett	319
Fox, Patrick	175	Feller, Chas.	331
Franklin, A.	178	Flack, C.	339
Franklin, Wm.	179	Falsin, Aug.	340
Fountain, R. A.	179	Floyd, R. H.	345
Franklin, J. M.	180	Frisbie, E. C.	346
French, John C.	185	Forester, Chas.	362
Flanakin, John	190	Forester, Mrs. E.	362
Fest, Henry	199	Fanning, J. G.	362
Fisk, James N.	211	Foster, J. J.	365
Field, Seaman	211	Foster, J. W.	368
Forbes, J. A.	213	Foster, James T.	368
Fink, W. M.	214	Freeman, Feanklin	372
Fonda, J. B.	231		
Griner, H. W.	8	Gerdis, Henry,	41
Griner, N. J.	8	Grosenbacher, John	43
Griner, A. J.	8	Gerdes, Gerd	46
Griner, H. C.	8	Grell, T. Otto	48
Gibson, Mrs. S.	21	Gerdes, John H.	52
Goldberg, C. F.	25	Gohlson, A. H.	55
Guly, Valentine	28	Gibbons, Emory	56
Gross, Roman	34	Gibson, Mrs. S. T.	57
Guitzcit, Fr.	37	Gabrisch, Gervas	79
Grunnewald, Mrs. Teresa	38	Gawlick, John	79

INDEX.

NAMES.	PAGES.	NAMES.	PAGES.
Goode, Wm. R.	83	Gembler, Christian	214
Gilbert, R. B.	85	Goll, Jacob	214
Gouger, H. A.	86	Giddings, G. H.	219
Garza, Frailan de la	87	Gray, Mrs. S.	226
Goodwin, B.	87	Gray, Jas.	227
Garza, Casamero	93	Gray, Wm.	227
Garza, Francisco de la	93	Gray, Mrs. Acmonia	227
Garza, Henriquez	94	Gray, Miss Mary	227
Gil, Miguil	95	Gugger, Anton	229
Gil, Ygnacio	96	Geier, Wm.	230
Gonzalez, Dimas	96	Grimm, Christian	234
Gonzales, Antonio	96	Gelven, Jasper	238
Grover, D. C.	100	Grobe, Henry	238
Grover, Geo. W., or agent	101	Geske, Henry	240
Grover, Eugene	105	Goodloe, A. G.	242
Gates, W. N.	128	Gillespie, Mrs. C. A.	244
Gilleland, G. D.	130	Goodwin, Ben.	247
Goin, Rayborn	131	Gohmart, Julius,	252
Gardner, Jos.	143	Gohlke, Fred.	254
Gardner, A. F.	143	Galle, Charles	255
Gardner, J. E.	143	Gerhardt, Peter	255
Gross, J. J.	147	Gerhardt, Charles	255
Grobs, Francis	149	Grafton, W. & S. B.	256
George, E. Ben.	153	Gohlke, John G.	258
George, Carl	156	Gaebler, Charles	258
Gass, Andres	158	Gentsche, Mrs. Julia	259
Goodwin, Mrs. E. C.	164	Grun, Jacob	260
Gildea, J. E., or agent	164	Grun, L. P.	261
Givens, Mathew	172	Gohlke, Rinhold	261
Gamble, Wm.	172	Goehring, Mrs. H.	261
Gallagher, Patrick,	173	Gohlke, John F.	262
Gussett, Miss Jo.	174	Goehring, August	262
Gallagher, B.	174	Gohlke, Johann	263
Gallagher, Thos.	175	Gohmert, Mrs. Justine	263
Grover, Jas. M.	175	Gohmert, Rudolph	268
Gembler, Jacob	190	Grun, John	268
Gil, Manuel	193	Golly, Miss Cath.	278
Garcia, Leandro	195	Golly, Anton	279
Gallardo, Juan M.	196	Grunewald, Joseph	279
Gillis, G. W.	198	Gentke, Charles	279
Gillis, M.	198	Greenly, J. H.	284
Gillis, Mrs. E.	198	Gentry, W. H.	294
Gembler, Christian	201	Gill, Thos.	296
Gillett, J. S.	204	Gray, Mrs. Jane	297
Garcia, Jose Antonio de la	207	Garcia, Ramon	306
Garcia, Jose Miguel de la	207	Garcia, Francisco	307
Gardner, T. G.	208	Garcia, Allahandro	307
Gayle, B. B.	211	Garcia, Luis	307
Gallagher, Peter	213	Gibbs, Jas. B.	310
Gallagher, Peter & Edward	213	Gibb, Jas.	310
Geiser, J. G	214	Givens, Mrs. A.	314

NAMES.	PAGES.	NAMES.	PAGES.
Gaffney, Owen	325	Gillespie, Mrs. M.	360
Gomes, B.	328	Gillespie, J. C.	360
Giles, T. A.	338	Gillett, Roswell	362
Gill, R. J.	346	Gillett, B. B.	363
Gipson, J. R.	347	Gay, W. M.	364
Gillespie, Mrs. E.	360	Guinn, N. W.	367
Hughs, James	8	Huschen, Diedrich	42
Harrison, T. H.	8	Hartung, Julius	43
Hannahan, Thos.	9	Harper, W. H.	44
Hannahan, Mary	11	Harper, John L.	44
Hill, John	11	Harper, G. W.	44
Hammers, Heirs	12	Harper, Mrs. Ann L.	44
Hiler, W. S.	14	Huchinson, W. S.	45
Hay, George	21	Heyen, John	46
Hay, Mrs. J.	21	Heien, Wm.	51
Haywood, L.	21	Hodges, Daniel	61
Hoffman, A.	22	Haskins, R. F.	64
Harrington, J. W.	22	Hutchison, Wm	80
Hayduk, Thos.	24	Hutchison, W. O.	82
Haby, Andres	25	Harper, G. F.	84
Haby, Ambrogo	26	Harper, E. S.	85
Haass, Valentine	26	Harper, Charles	86
Heineman, Peter	26	Hitchings, G. W.	88
Hoffman, Nicholas	27	Houston, G. J.	89
Heuchling, Julius	27	Houston, Russell	89
Haby, Jacob	28	Houston, G. J. & R.	89
Haldy, Miss Mary	28	Hernandez, M.	90
Hoffmann, John	28	Herrera, M. C.	91
Haass, Henry	31	Holdusen, Henry	92
Haby, Mrs. Martha	31	Herrera, Raffella	92
Haass, Geo.	31	Hernandez, Cresencio	97
Haass, Mrs. A. M.	31	Hudson, R. B.	97
Huth, Louis	32	Hayes, W. B.	98
Harr, Mrs. Minerva	33	Hynes, John	98
Haass, G. L.	34	Holt, Vincent	104
Haby, Nicholas	34	Hynes, Wm.	105
Haberly, John	35	Howel, Flint, & Tumlinson,	105
Herfurth, Samuel	36	Hayden, J. T.	110
Herfurth, John	36	Harrison, L. B.	118
Haass, Philip	37	Hill, Miss Francis	119
Haby, Louis	38	Hall, F. & Bro.	121
Haass, Fredrick	39	Henshaw, John	125
Heath, S. P.	39	Harrison, James C.	125
Heath, Louis	39	Hilburn, R.	126
Heath, Jesse	39	Harrison, J. M.	131
Haller, Fredrick	41	Harris, L. B.	132
Hartmann, Henry	41	Hill, John	133

NAMES.	PAGES.	NAMES.	PAGES.
Hay, Nathaniel	136	Haw, John	219
Hay, Mrs. Eliza	139	Hans, Leonhard	221
Hoffman, Joseph	140	Hutchison, Isaac	223
Hay, Silas	145	Hutchison, O. P.	223
Herring, Jacob	150	Hutchison, W. C.	223
Hirshleber, Julius	151	Herndon & Kerr	225
Haag, Mrs. Martias	152	Herndon, J. H. or agt.	226
Hohmann, C.	152	Heineman, Peter	226
Haseldanz, Michael	153	Haberman, H.	228
Hoffmann, T. B.	154	Hines, W. O.	231
Hoitckamp, Henriech	155	Hale, W. A.	231
Heidrech, Jacob	155	Hines, E. C.	231
Hilger, C. L.	155	Hawkins, W. L.	233
Hitzfelder, L.	156	Hoffman, L. H.	235
Horne, Peter	157	Hoffman, John	236
Haas, J. J.	158	Hoffman, Peter	237
Haas, August	158	Hoffman, Henrich	237
Hirholzer, Joseph	158	Hild, Geo.	298
Hoflinz, C.	160	Hutmacher, Carl	238
Herring, Curtis	163	Hellmann, Robt.	242
Harrison, T. R.	165	Hamilton, Wm. S.	242
Healy, John	165	Henderson, Mrs. S. R.	247
Heritage, J. T. or agt.	166	Humphries, Jas.	249
Harrison, James	167	Hains, Mrs. Carolina	251
Hinton, Mrs. Ann J.	171	Harper, M. A.	251
Hunter & Cox.	172	Hoppe, Frantz	254
Heermann, Theo. & Bro.	184	Haruff, Mrs. E. J.	255
Hernandez, Jesus, sr.	184	Hahn, W.	257
Hernandez, Jesus	184	Hahn, C. H.	260
Herrera, Manuel	186	Homrighausen, Peter	261
Herrera, Blas, jr.	186	Holdeman, David	261
Herrera, Bonito	187	House, F.	261
Herrera, Blas, sr.	187	Humphreys, G. W.	262
Horn, Anton	191	Hennig, C. F. W.	266
Herf, F.	191	Heisjig, C. H.	266
Henson & Bro.	192	Hardy, D. N.	267
Harris, C. S.	193	Heard, Jasper N.	268
Herrera, Romana	194	Heard, H.	269
Herrera, Jose Maria	195	Harrell, Miss M.	270
Hubert, Albert	195	Hearn, W. D.	271
Herrera, Manuel, sr.	196	Holzapfel, Gustave	271
Hernandez, Peter	197	Heard, Joel B.	272
Huron, Bibian	197	Hoffman, Henry	272
Hernandez, Peter, jr.	198	Holzapfel, Ed.	274
Herman, Gegoria	200	Hoffer, Antone	274
Hopfelt, C.	205	Hamilton, J. R.	275
Huebner, James	205	Hamilton, Alex.	276
Hoerner, George	214	Hans, Ambrose	277
Howard, G. T.	215	Hinuber, W. V.	277
Harris, Amos	217	Haun, Adolph	279

NAMES.	PAGES	NAMES.	PAGES
Hotz, Anton	280	Henderson, F. V.	336
Hiller, Michael	282	Hermann, John	337
Hiller, Fredk	282	Hofheinz, C.	337
Hord, Jesse	284	Harbour, Mrs. M. E.	337
Howell, T. F.	288	Hoerner, John	338
Hassell, Jesse	292	Herbest, Sophia	338
Helper, Miss E.	293	Haérter, C.	340
Hoff, Wm.	294	Heuermann, Wm.	340
Hargrave, Miss C.	297	Heiner, Chas.	343
Hargrave, O.	298	Hall, S. N.	345
Housman, H.	300	Hancock, W. M.	349
Hadt, Henry	301	Henry, G. W.	351
Hobbs, James	311	Hoover, N. J.	354
Hobbs, Wm.	311	Hanson, C. J.	363
Holbrook, W. W.	316	Hall, H. F.	363
Holbrook, W. W. agt.	316	Holmes, W. F. M.	365
Howell, J. M. & J. C	317	Hurt, E. R.	365
Huddlestor, Mrs. E.	318	Harper, W. F.	365
Hardiman, R. B.	325	Hubbard, S. A.	367
Hart, P.	325	Hestor, R. H.	369
Hinrichson, J. H.	325	Harper Mrs. Jane	369
Harper, L.	333	Hesson, Mrs. Harriet	370
Hasckamp, G. H.	335	Hand, J. B.	372
Harz, F.	336		
Iltis, John	34	Inselman, H. J.	221
Iltis, Seraphim	35	Inselmann, J. G.	221
Ihnken, Gerhard	37	Irvin, Mrs. Sarah	246
Irvin, P. B.	104	Irvin, W. C.	246
Imhoff, Henry	162	Ingenhuett, H.	342
Juretzky, F.	24	Jimenes, Juan	96
Jones, John A.	24	Jones, Wm.	107
Jungmann, Peter	26	Jones, A. C., or agent	112
Jungmann, Mrs. R.	30	Jolley, James	118
Jungmann, Mrs. C.	30	Jolley, Miss N. J.	118
Jung, Z.	38	Jones, Urial	120
Johnson, T. J.	50	Jones, Irvin	126
Johnson, G. S.	50	Jones, Philip	157
Johnzon, John	56	John, J.	159
Jones, Oliver	57	Johnson, R. B.	165
Jones, Wm.	58	Jackson, W. H.	183
Jones, J. M.	66	James, John	184
Jimenes, Francisco	84	Jaques, W. B.	185
Jimenes, Melchor	90	Jecker, Celestin	186
Jimenes, Antonio	94	Jones, A. D.	192

NAMES.	PAGES.	NAMES.	PAGES.
Jaegly, Jos.	201	Jasper, Eliza Ann	224
Jones, Jesse	213	Jacobs, Geo. W.	255
Jagge, G.	214	Jacobs, A. J.	256
Jeffries, Mrs. J.	215	Jdeus, Fokke	278
Jeffries, W.	215	Jdeus, Simon	279
Joues, S. C.	215	Junker, John G.	281
Jones, Mrs. Charlotte	215	Jones, Jas. F.	283
Johnson, L. W.	217	Jackson, Mrs. H. A.	291
Johnson & McDaniel	217	Jones, C. M.	299
Johnson, Mrs. Cynthia	217	Jacobs, Henry	300
Johnson, Virgil	217	Jordan, P. A.	300
Johnson, W. D.	217	Joclin, John	307
Johnson, H. C.	218	Joclin, Dicodena	307
Johnson, Miss M. A.	218	Joups, Joseph	316
Jones, T. S.	221	Jones, G. F.	325
Jungmann, John	222	Johnson, A. B.	349
Kelley, L. C.	14	Kowolick, John	79
Kennedy, John	15	Kelly, R. A.	80
Klappenbach, A.	22	Kelly, W. G.	81
Kindla, John	22	King, John R.	85
Kalka, Casper	22	Kilgore, J. J.	86
Kalka, Joseph	22	Kennedy, W. A.	108
Koenig, Jacob	27	Kotula, Miss Mary	118
Ketchum, C. V.	28	Kotula, Joseph	119
Kempf, Joseph	30	Kelly, Wm.	126
Kohl, John	32	Kennard, J. N.	135
Kreissle, John	33	Kennard, N. G.	135
Koenig, Jacob	33	Klempke, Mrs. A.	139
Krust, Joseph	34	Koester, Theo.	147
Krust, Miss Jennie	34	Koch, Carl	148
Kappart, Frank	38	Katterle, John	150
Ketchum, Mrs. S. E.	38	Kneeiper, Christian	155
King, Isaac	43	Kneeiper, Peter	155
King, Horace P.	44	Katerle, Jacob	156
Kelly, W. M.	55	Kraft, Henry	158
Kelly, John	55	Kablemacher H.	159
Kelly, N. L.	55	Knibbe, Deitrich	160
King, John L.	62	Krause, George	162
King, James P.	63	Kreugener, E. Q.	162
Kalus, F.	74	King, J. G.	168
Kuhnel, John	74	Kivlin, Mathew	170
Keller, Dominik	75	Kyle, W. J.	177
Kotzur, Frank	75	Kennedy, G. W.	179
Kroll, Frank	76	Knight, George	183
Kniesky, Albert	78	Kablemacher, John	190
Kolenda, Dominik	78	Knox, W. B.	191
Keriss, Joseph	79	Kuntz, Andre	200
Kaspzick, Albert	79	Kuntz, Sebastian	200

NAMES.	PAGES.	NAMES.	PAGES
Kaiserling, C. F.	200	Kirlicks, John	259
Kerr, W. P.	203	Kirlicks, Wm.	259
Kerr, W. H.	203	Krage, August	259
Kerr, Mrs. N. R. S.	203	Kirlicks, Christopher	260
Kerr, I. N.	204	Korschal, John	260
Knight, Theo.	207	Kauffman, Nicholas	262
Kenny, John	212	Korth, Mrs. Louise	263
Kenny, Thos.	213	King, W. F. & Bro.	268
Kingsbury, W. G.	214	Kelso, John R.	269
Krempkau, C. G.	220	Kriksi, Fred	272
Keller, Joseph	223	Kleberg, Robt.	277
Krtiezka, Joseph sr.	225	Koenig, A.	279
Krtiezka, Joseph	225	Kohler, Antoine	281
Kieser, Carl	225	Killebrew, W. B.	284
King, H. C.	228	Killebrew, G. W.	284
Kraut, Fredk	229	Kuykendall, J. W.	291
Koopsel, M.	234	Kurkendall, J. B.	291
Kurre, Heinrich	235	Kuykendall, Miss J.	313
Krueger, Carl	236	Kuykendall, Wm.	313
Koemer, Christopher	236	Kuykendall, Mrs. E. M.	313
Knetsch, Wm,	237	Kroeger, H.	324
Klein, Valentine	237	Kellett, John	325
Kurre, Ludwig	238	Kutscher,	332
Kingore, J. T.	253	Kallenberg, John	332
Kroschel, Lewis	254	Koch, Anton	336
Klotz, Ludwig	254	Kendall, G. W.	337
Kilbassa, Peter	255	Kapp, E.	340
Koch, Mrs. Mary	258	Karger, C.	343
Kuast, Julius,	259	King, Mrs. Emma	356
Lease, W. B.	9	Little, J. M.	61
Lewis, Jessie	11	Lawhon, L. S.	62
Lakey, N. M. C.	15	Lies, Charles	67
Lakey, John	15	Littleton, John	70
Lockart, W. A.	20	Lipscomb, L. S.	72
Laxon, Mrs. Elizabeth	22	Little, Mrs. Sarah	72
Lamon, John	29	Lawhon, Mrs. S. M.	72
Lytle, John T.	33	Labus, Adam	74
Lee, James	33	Licy, Frank	77
Loesberg, John	38	Lopez, Florentina	90
Leinweber, George,	41	Lynch, Tho's	100
Loug, S. A.	42	Lockhart, C. L.	111
Leinweber, August	43	Lee, J. N.	112
Leinweber, John	45	Leahy, Wm.	115
Long, A. J.	49	Little, J. E.	116
Long, W. H.	49	Long, T. A.	121
Langford, M. H,	56	Long, C. Y.	122
Lee, Oliver	57	Lewis, L.	140
Lyons, D. C.	60	Lindheimer, F. J.	149

INDEX.

NAMES.	PAGES.	NAMES.	PAGES.
Leffler, Christian	155	Lundscien, Mrs. Anne	256
Latham Louis C.	166	Lempke, F.	265
Latham, James	169	Ludwik, Joseph	265
Latham, Jas. R.	169	Lundscin,	266
Latham, John	170	Lord, Geo.	271
Lewis, S. W.	174	Lobel, Jacob	273
Lowe, James	179	Luder, Pantaleon	279
Lane, A.	180	Linsey, S. R.	285
Linn, Jacob	185	Lunsford, Hiram	285
Lange, W.	186	Ludeback, Y. N.	285
Long, John	188	Lacky, Hershell	288
Leal, Manuel	189	Lott, R. or agt.	295
Losoyo, Domingo	196	Ladwyk, Joseph	301
Leslie, A. J.	198	Larema, F.	312
Langwell, H. A.	207	Lary, Martines	326
Lewis, Nat	208	Lewis, W. C.	329
Lege, Charles	208	Lewis & McSween	329
Lombrana, Antonio	210	Lindsey, J. B.	329
Lackey, A. J.	210	Lock, W. J.	333
Lane, E. D.	211	Lacy, J. H.	333
Lorenz, Anton	214	Lindner, M.	339
Lopez, Benito	215	Lussmann, G. H.	339
Lackey, Mrs. M.	217	Lowrence, W. A.	344
Lytle, Wm.	219	Lowrence, D. B.	344
Luckey, W.	223	Lemond, C.	345
Lann, Mrs. Rhoda	231	Lambert, A.	348
Lann, Miss Sarah F.	231	Lambert, Thos.	348
Lann, Miss Minerva L.	231	Loyd, M. T.	348
Linne, Earnst	239	Lambert, S. B.	353
Leihner, Johannette	240	Lemmond, J. W.	354
Lann, Burrel	241	Lookingbill, J. M.	358
Lewis, Riley	244	Lookingbill, G. W.	365
Lyons, Patrick	245	Little, M. T.	365
Lambert Mrs. Mary	252	Littlefield, P. B.	366
Mckinney, T. N.	8	Miller, J. B.	24
Miller, S. R.	10	Mazyerock, Thomas	25
McKinney, J. E.	11	Mehring, Louis	27
McKinney, J. T.	11	Moore, Lon.	27
Mckinney, Eliza C.	11	Macar. Joseph	30
Mckinney, C. C.	18	Montel, Charles de	31
Miles, O. B.	20	Mangold, George, sén.	32
Monroe, David	20	Mangold, George, jr.	32
Miller, T. L.	22	Mullen, W. C.	33
Mott, Samuel C.	22	Merian, John	34
Miller, Thomas	23	Mann, Joseph	35
Miller, Mrs. Martha	23	Mechler, Richard	35
McKay, H. C.	23	Moore, D. B.	39
Moravets, Joseph	23	Moore, H. M	39

INDEX.

NAMES.	PAGES.	NAMES.	PAGES.
Mechler, August	40	McIver, John	111
Mumme, Ludwig	41	McClanahan, G. W.	712
McLamore, Daniel	41	May, H. R.	112
Meyer, Albg	43	McCollom, G. B.	116
McDonald, W. G.	46	Marsden, T. H.	116
Malone, T. P.	48	Martin, A. G.	118
Marques, Remi	48	Martin, G. Henry	118
Martin, Andres	50	Martin, Mrs. Mary	118
McLamore, J. B.	51	McCoy, Simpson	119
Munnink, Fred.	52	McMains, J. W.	120
McCombs, Mrs. M. A.	53	Mansfield, F. M.	122
Myrick, Wm.	54	McMains, Andrew	123
Mayer, F.	54	Musgrave, Bennett	126
Miller, J. W.	54	Musgrave, Calvin	126
Miller, R. C.	54	Musgrave, J. Q.	129
Miller, G. W.	54	Morris, Wm., sen.	135
McCrabb, Joseph	61	Morris, Wm., jun.	136
Mayfield, W. H.	65	Martin, Mrs. Louisa	136
Mayfield, E. A.	65	Morris, Spencer	136
Mitchell, Wm.	66	Marshall, W.	137
McCrabb, Mrs. Mary	66	Martin, Wm. F.	138
McLane, H. H.	68	Martin, John	138
McLane, W. J.	68	Mangum, J. S.	144
McLane, J. A.	68	Mangum, W. Z.	144
Moy, Lucas	73	Mangum, G. M.	144
McLane, H. B.	75	Mangum, N. T.	144
Minka, Frank	77	McKinney, Julius	145
Morzygemba, Thomas	78	Mather, Samuel	148
Morzygemba, Joseph	78	Meyer, Conrad	148
Morzygemba, John	78	Markwardt, P.	157
Morzygemba, Mrs. Mary	79	McIntosh, Wm.	163
Mahoney, Florence	83	McIntosh, Mrs.	163
Morris, James S.	83	Minter, W.	164
McDaniel, G. H.	85	Meriman, Walter	166
Martinez, C.	86	McWhorter, S. S.	168
McDaniel, J.	90	Murray, James	170
Mirando, Macedonia	91	Mass, Sam'l	171
Montoyo, Mrs. T.	94	Marshall, John	172
Menchaca, Jose M.	94	Miller, S. G.	176
Menchaca, Barnabe	95	Murphy, Dan.	183
Montoyo, Hilario	95	McCulloch, Sam'l	186
Mullen, Ira, or agent	98	Mitchell, W. J.	187
Mullen, Mrs. J. or agent	99	Mitchell, Frank	187
Miller, Wm.	183	Mushall, George	190
May, David R.	104	McDona, Geo.	192
Mullen, F. J. or agent	106	Martinez, Jose D.	193
McColom, J. M.	106	Martinez, Aniceto	195
Maddry, James	109	McMulligan, Con.	197
Mitchell, Mrs. E. E.	110	Metzdorff, Chas.	200
Martin, Archibald	110	Martinez, Jose	201

NAMES.	PAGES.	NAMES.	PAGES.
Miller, Chas.	202	Moaller, Christian	280
Mudd, Geo. W.	203	Mumbrauer, H.	291
Mitchell, Barney	205	Mack, L. F. or agt.	283
Marnoch, G. F.	207	Mellews, Mrs. M. H.	284
McCann, J.	207	Murry, F. E.	285
Mitchell, Asa	208	Middleton, Charley	285
Menjares, Francisco	209	McCampbell, J. W.	287
Moye, Albert	212	McCampbell, W. S.	290
Moudragon, E.	215	Middleton, B. F.	290
Mondragon, Francis	215	McDaniel W. J.	291
McOlusky, Pat.	216	Miller, J. G. or J. P.	293
Merick, M. L.	219	Middleton, S. P.	297
Meyer, Jos.	221	Middleton, Miss M. E.	297
Mann, John L.	222	Meyer, Wm.	299
Mann, Valentine	222	Maddux, James	302
Meyer, Seraphim	226	Mussett, W. S. K.	303
Marty, Sebastian	226	Mussett, Tyrey	304
Montez, Antonio	227	McCoy, Dennis	304
Montez, Manuel	227	Mann, Mrs. E. L.	305
Montez, Alejos	227	Mann, Mrs. E. S.	305
Maltsburger, G. W.	229	McLaughlin, A.	306
Miller, John G.	230	Mindieta, Leonisio	307
McGee, John S.	233	Miller, R. J.	308
Monk, Christopher	234	Miller, R. C.	308
Maurer, C.	237	Merrimon, Elizabeth	309
Molberg, Mrs. Margaret	238	McIntyre, D.	310
Mourin, J. P.	243	McMurray, Jas.	312
Mays, Watkins V.	246	McGrew, R. W.	313
Mays, Mrs. Anna D.	246	McGrew & Ragland	314
Morrison, W. C.	246	McGrew, J. & H.	314
Miller, Jacob	247	McGree, W. P.	315
Morris, Wm.	248	Martin, Robt.	319
Morris, R. W.	249	McCarty, J. R.	323
McKinney, W. J.	250	McGloin, A. & P.	326
Murray, David,	252	McGowin, T.	326
Mahust, Henry	253	McWhorter, D. W.	326
Metz, Peter	256	McSween, John	330
Metz, Miss L.	257	McFaddin, E. A.	342
Metz, Miss Amelia	257	Mills, H. H.	347
Martin, Heinrich	259	Mitchell, N.	349
Mahnest, John	261	May, Morris	349
Menn, Heinrich	263	Miller, Mrs. C.	351
Metz, Antonio	265	Martin, J. F.	352
Meun, Fredk	265	Mill, John	353
McFarland, Mrs. M. C.	267	Mathieu, J. T.	353
McAllister, A.	271	Morrow, Mrs. E.	353
McMillan, Mrs. Julia	273	Mitchell G. D.	354
Murphree, Miss A. E.	275	McAda, W. S.	354
Myer, Adolph	277	Mathews, T. N.	354
Munch, Nichlas	279	Moorey, J. G. & Bro.	357

NAMES.	PAGES.	NAMES.	PAGES.
Murray, James M.	360	Morris, Alfred	364
Murray, Mrs. E.	360	McGuffin, W. B.	365
Murray, J. R.	361	Morris, E. F.	366
McPeters, John	361	McCoy, C.	366
McPeters, Thomas	361	McCoy, Mrs. C.	366
McPeters, Geo.	361	McCoy, P. C.	366
Marcum, F. M.	362	Moore, Mrs. S. H.	367
Mangum, J. M.	363	McCoy, L. S.	367
Mangum, Miss E. T.	363	McCoy, Texas	367
Mangum, L. L.	363	McCoy, Mrs. S.	367
McCoy, Joseph	364	Monroe, James	369
Nimmo, G. T.	15	Newberry, J. C.	172
Norton, Miss Esther J.	17	Newberry, H. B.	172
Noonan, G. H.	25	Newberry, G. W.	172
Notter, Joseph	32	Nichols, Mrs. M.	173
Naegelin, Michael jr.	33	Noel, Geo. W.	193
Naegelin, Michael sr.	35	Navarro, Luciano	201
Niggle, Ferdinand	36	Neighbors, E. A. Est. of	204
Nietenhofer, John	45	Neighbors & Serna	205
Nietenhofer, Adolph	51	Nuchol, Lewis W.	210
Ney, Joseph	55	Newton, W. C.	211
Ney & Reily	55	Nagle, John	234
Newman, A. R.	64	Newton, D. C.	248
Newberry, J. D.	70	Newton, Jas.	248
Newman, Mrs. R.	72	Newman, A. F.	276
Newman, J. A. jr.	82	Newcomer, A.	301
Nier, E.	85	Newcomer, F. G.	301
Nutt, John A.	99	Nance, Henry	301
New, J. B.	99	Noakes, T. J.	310
Nutt, R. E.	100	Newsom, M.	314
Notgrass, Mrs. A.	122	Nimitz, C. H.	331
Navarro, J. Antonio	122	Nations, A. J.	346
Neal, J. D.	123	Newsom, R.	349
Neal, J. P.	123	Nations, James	355
Nichols, Wm. N.	125	Nations, James & Robt.	355
Neill, Sam'l H.	128	Nations, J. T.	355
Neill, B. F.	128	Nichols, L.	356
Neill, Robt.	134	Nowlin, S. H.	363
O'Gi, Louis	11	Oefinger, John	49
O'Brion, Wilson	17	Oltman, O. N.	51
Oberski, E.	23	Oltman, A. N.	51
Onion, Joseph	23	Opelia, Anton	73
Owings, J. R.	31	Opelia, Anna	74
Oefinger, Paul	42	Opelia, Jakob	77
Oefinger, Andres	43	Opelia, Nicholas	77
Oltman, Fredrick	46	Opiela, John	77

INDEX.

NAMES.	PAGES.	NAMES.	PAGES.
Olynik, Mrs Marie	78	Obst, Gotleb	190
Osman, John	82	Owings & Knox,	191
Orosco, Ysidro	84	Owings, L. S.	191
Ortiz, Bartolo	87	Ortiz, Bruno	197
Odom, Mrs. D. D.	108	Odom, T. L.	198
O'Brion, E.	118	Ogden, D. C.	210
Oden, A. L.	130	Olivera, Placido	216
Oden, M. D.	130	Oatman, P. S.	218
Oden, T. S.	130	Oatman, P. S.,	229
Oden, Mrs. Caroline	130	Orth, John	236
Oden, Mrs. Eliza	135	Orth, Jacob	236
Owens, Wm.	138	Odom, Justus	251
Oppermann, Fred.	140	Odom, Mrs. Martha	251
Owen, Mrs. Malinda B.	150	Odom, Mrs. L.	268
Ohealey, Michael	166	Ott, Antonio,	278
Osborn, Z. H.	166	Owens, B.	288
O'Reily, H. J.	172	O'Neill, W.	350
O'Neal, Terry	188	O'Neill, H.	366
Pulliam, W. H.	15	Peacock, T. J.	85
Patterson, G. W., sen.	15	Potts, E.	85
Patterson, John C.	15	Peres, Jose Antonio	85
Patterson, G. W. jr.	15	Peres, Jesus	87
Patterson, W. B.	16	Peres, Antonio	90
Patterson, G. R.	16	Pickett, A. G.	90
Patterson, N. M. C.	16	Peres, Juan	91
Patterson, J. W.	16	Pontoga, Esteven	93
Patterson, J. J. H.	16	Prue, Mrs. Narcissa	96
Pulliam, B. A.	18	Park, J. W. or agt.	102
Pafford, W. E.	19	Park, Wm. or agent	102
Pafford, Randolph	19	Parsons, Hugh	104
Pafford, T. M.	19	Phelps, J. A.	105
Phillips, J. W.	20	Parker, Mrs. E. L.	108
Poor, Joseph	23	Parchman, W. M.	109
Pingenot, Peter F.	32	Parker, Willis	111
Petrerict, Leonhard	37	Palmer, C. B.	114
Paul, James	38	Phelps, Mrs. S.	114
Poehler, Henry	46	Perkins. J.	117
Porter, Wm.	57	Perkins, Jesse	117
Postert, Jacob	58	Perkins, Cader	117
Pulliam, Mrs. A.	61	Perkins, Joshua	117
Parker, Mrs. Nancy	61	Palacio, Juan	124
Puckett, Thos. H.	63	Palasio, Janario	124
Porter, George	66	Props, T. H.	132
Perryman, S.	68	Parchman, Lemuel	133
Puckett & McLane	69	Parchman, W. & Martin	133
Puckett, L. D.	70	Peacock, James T.	135
Piegza, Joseph	75	Props, H. J.	135
Pawelick, Losenz	79	Padia, Antonio	134
Peres, Jose Maria	84	Preston W. F.	147

INDEX.

NAMES.	PAGES.	NAMES.	PAGES.
Pape, Andres	149	Post, Henry	266
Pape, Conrad, sen.	149	Puckett, S. M.	269
Pape, Andres, jun.	152	Peavy, D. B.	279
Pape, Conrad, jun.	156	Porter, W. J.	280
Pape, Wm.	156	Prusky, Jacob	281
Pfeuffer, George	159	Power, Richard	283
Pugh, Thomas	165	Paten, Mrs. E.	287
Pugh, B.	165	Percy, Mrs. M. J.	287
Pugh, Wm.	167	Phillips, Mrs. Annie	288
Pugh, P.	174	Prescott, Chas.	288
Pearce, S.	180	Prescott, B. C.	290
Pena, Ignacio	184	Power, M. H.	292
Paschal, I. A.	186	Parsons, Robt.	295
Presnall, Harrison	188	Paxton, Mrs. P.	298
Pendleton, G.	189	Preston, Lewis	306
Perez, Ignacio	189	Durham & Richardson	309
Piper, August	190	Perkins, Jas.	309
Pue, E. B. & S. B.	199	Power, Jas.	315
Power, Charles	201	Power, Felipe	315
Poor, D. M.	206	Plummer, Mrs. J. E.	315
Poor, F. S.	206	Pierpont, Wm.	316
Park, W. R.	210	Polan, J.	327
Pue, E. B.	216	Phillip, J. W.	334
Pue, S. B.	216	Phillip, J.	334
Pancoast, J.	217	Pfeifer, Aug.	334
Pearce, Mrs. Eliza	224	Patton, J. M.	335
Plehwe, Geo.	229	Patton, S. B.	335
Park, Mrs. A. P. A. T	231	Patton, C. A.	335
Pfannstiel, Aug.	235	Perner, F.	340
Pfannstiel, Wm.	235	Power, Benj.	345
Pfannstiel, Fredk.	238	Price, J. T.	346
Pfennstiel, F. D.	238	Pierson, W. M.	346
Pfeil, Jacob	242	Putman, John,	347
Perryman, T. J.	243	Putman, S. V.	347
Polley, J. H.	247	Passmore, B. A.	350
Polley, J. B.	247	Putman, Wm. sr.	352
Praytor, W. B.	252	Putman, Wm. jr.	352
Pritz, Fred	253	Pease, Samuel	356
Peace, Mrs. R.	254	Pierson, E. T.	362
Powel, Houston	255	Pierce, G. W.	366
Peace, M.	255	Parson, S. S.	369
Powel, Sam'l	264	Preston, L. A.	369
Pritz, Mrs. Ann	266	Pierson, William	371
Porter, John T.	266		
Quesenberry, J. T.	188	Quinney, Mrs. R.	571
Quinney, L.	371		

INDEX

NAMES.	PAGES.	NAMES.	PAGES.
Richeson, D. T.	9	Roberts, W. D.	101
Reynolds, W. M.	10	Ryan, J. P.	104
Reynolds & Adams	10	Robeson, R. M.	109
Roony, F.	16	Rawlings, F. P.	112
Robinson, Mrs. E.	17	Rawlings, Miss M. L.	112
Rodriguez, J. P.	23	Rawlings, Miss E. B.	112
Rugh, Daniel	24	Rawlings, Miss S. V.	113
Rine, Mrs. Mary	24	Robertston, Mrs. S. J.	113
Renken, H. T.	28	Rawlings, Jas. B.	113
Redus, George	44	Rawlings, H. A.	113
Redus, John	44	Ryan, H. C.	113
Reitzer, John	45	Ryan, Mrs. L. or agt.	113
Reitzer, Ambrose,	45	Robeson, J. W.	115
Rackley, Wilson	46	Ryan, James	116
Riff, Jacob	46	Ryan, Henry	116
Rieden, Mrs. D.	48	Ryman, Jacob	121
Roelf, Frederick	49	Rodriguez, Simon	122
Redus, William	51	Robinson, S. S. or agt.	122
Robbins, G. W.	52	Rogers, Wm. or agt.	122
Redus, George	53	Rodriguez, Senon	123
Rienhardt, John	57	Rodriguez, Manuel	124
Russell, Chas.	58	Reider, Simon	124
Rhymes, G. W.	58	Ribas, M.	127
Rhymes, Mrs. C. A.	58	Russell, Mrs. M. J.	130
Reagan, W. B.	60	Russell, Chas. S.	130
Rhymes, J. F.	61	Rodriguez, H.	136
Rhymes, W. J.	61	Ridgeway, Mrs. C.	138
Reagan, John M.	62	Ranbic, Aaron	140
Ricks, Mrs. Martha	65	Renarz, F. W.	147
Robertson, Joseph	66	Reinninger H.	151
Reese, T. J. C.	67	Renninger, Geo.	151
Reese, G. M.	67	Reinhardt, F.	151
Roark, W. G.	70	Remmler, Gabriel	161
Rabb, Thos.	71	Reest, Fredrick	162
Ratliff, R.	71	Robinson, Alfred	170
Rose, P. H.	71	Rainy, J. W.	175
Ratliff, J. J.	72	Rivas, Edwardo	184
Rzeppa, John	73	Rodriguez, Juan	189
Rabstien, John	75	Ruiz, Francisco	189
Rosser, John	76	Ruiz, Eugenio	189
Rosser, B. F.	77	Ripstein, Sebastian	189
Rutherford, C.	86	Raux, Emile	193
Ruiz, Bernideno	86	Rodriguez, Catrina	195
Rector. C.	89	Reynolds, David	196
Roxo, Jose M.	91	Rhodes, F. K.	205
Ruiz, Jose A.	92	Rodriguez, José Marie	209
Rodriguez, J. N.	92	Ruiz, Alejandro M.	209
Reyes, Pedro	97	Ruiz, Maria Sanfrosa	217
Rupe, Mrs. Cleopatra	99	Rzeppa, Emanuel	220
Robeson, Mrs. D.	100	Rzeppa, Matilda	220

INDEX.

NAMES.	PAGES	NAMES.	PAGES.
Rodriguez, Juan	226	Rives, James	282
Real, Adolph	231	Rush, S. M.	286
Rudeloff, F.	234	Reynolds, Miss C.	286
Reinhard, Frank	237	Rush, Peter jr.	287
Rathke, Carl	239	Rush, Miss M. A.	287
Rhodius, Mrs. O.	241	Rutherford, W. W.	296
Rhodes, A. H.	245	Rouse, F.	296
Reynolds, M. H.	245	Reynolds, Mrs. H.	296
Russell, W. R.	252	Reynolds, John P.	298
Rummel, Fredk	253	Rabbit, L.	300
Rattliff, Wm. R.	255	Riggs, W. C.	301
Reidesel, Ludwig	257	Runnels, Geo.	303
Riedel, M.	257	Rabb, John	304
Rattliff, Elija	261	Rabb, G. A. & T. L,	308
Roeder, J. V.	263	Rogers, L. M.	316
Range, John	265	Ryals, John	316
Rojes, Anastasio	266	Reeves, Wm.	317
Riedel, Mrs. Jo.	267	Ritche, E.	336
Riedel, Chas.	267	Rhodius, Christoph	341
Riedel, Joseph	268	Rhodius, Mrs. B.	341
Robison, J. W.	269	Ritchie, W. A.	348
Richter, J. H.	274	Riley, H.	348
Reinhardt, Jacob	274	Rogers, J. N.	354
Rochl Ferdinand	274	Rainey, T. F.	357
Rochl, Robt.	275	Rayborn, L. M.	357
Reinhardt, Louis	276	Reeves, A. C.	363
Rabke, Mrs. H.	278	Robbins, A. M.	368
Rath, Peter	280		
Smith, W. F.	9	Speyer, George	42
Shores, W. L.	9	Steigler, Got.	43
Stratton, N. L.	9	Schorobing, R.	47
Sanders, J. B.	11	Saathoff, Foke	48
Snow, G. P.	16	Sturm, John	49
Spears, Sam.	19	Schwerz, S.	50
Baner, P. D.	20	Smith, Mrs. M.	50
Sutherland, Joseph	24	Simpson, J. J.	51
Stephens, J. T.	24	Saathoff, M. M.	52
Schneider, Anton	29	Saathoff, John	52
Steinle, Brancis	29	Schulte, Frank	52
Saltner, Joseph	30	Smith, Mrs. L.	53
Schorp, Joseph	30	Smith, Wm.	55
Spattel, Mrs. Mary	32	Schumacher, A.	55
Schneider, Joseph	33	Snow, P. G.	57
Schmidt, Martin	38	Scogin, D. G.	59
Saathoff, Memke M.	41	Schmidt, J. L.	59
Steigler, Mrs. R.	41	Sullivan, J.	60
Steigler, Gottleib	42	Strickland, A. O. & J.	61
Schumacker, Wm.	42	Silvers, Hiram	62
Schumacker, Christian	42	Sumner, John	65

INDEX.

NAMES.	PAGES.	NAMES.	PAGES
Sullivan, John	66	Shutz, Ludwig	152
Short, J. L.	73	Simon, Sylvester	152
Skiles, J. R.	75	Schwab, Thomas	152
Skiles, Miss Mary	75	Schafer, Carl	153
Szebanik, Lorenz	75	Schmidt, Jacob	154
Sziegol, Joseph	76	Schmidt, Mrs. Maria	154
Sanches, Jose	77	Startz, Henry	154
Stirtz, John	78	Schwab, Valentine	154
Shott, Wm. F.	79	Schlader, Adam	155
Stannard, Harvy	80	Schuchart, Carl	155
Seguin, Mrs. T. F.	84	Simon, Martin	157
Santos, Nicolas de los	86	Syring, Mrs. Ann	157
Seguin, Mrs. G. F.	88	Smithson, B. F.	159
Scull, W. D.	89	Stahl, Jacob	159
Samora, Felipe	95	Smith, Mrs. M.H.	159
Sauseda, Pabla	95	Secrest, J. M.	160
Sanches, Decidro	97	Specht, Hans	161
Summerville, James	97	Schertz, Sebastian	161
Sullivan, Miss H.	98	Scheft, Charles	161
Smith, Tho's J.	98	Seegers, Jacob	161
Sedgewick, Ed.	99	Secrest, O. M.	162
Sullivan, D. W.	100	Shipp, P. F.	165
Spaulding, Ephraim H.	103	Smith, L.	168
Scott, Mrs. P.	106	Slorter, Waller	169
Seeligson, M.	108	Stephens, J. E.	170
Smith, S. H.	110	Shannon, Thomas	173
Steen, J. C.	110	Sheeren, Thos.	173
Scott, W. A.	114	Sheeren, Mrs. Mary	175
Scott, Tho's P.	114	Sheeren, Patrick	175
Scott, Miss Susan	114	Shipp, E. S.	176
Saltsman, Mrs. Sophia	118	Staples, W. W.	176
Saltsman, Frank	119	Sparks, Mrs. L. J.	178
Sotelo, Ygnacio sen.	123	Settle, J. A.	183
Sotelo, Ygnacio jun.	123	Smythe, Peyton	186
Saucero, Antonio	125	Stanfield, J. C.	187
Sherman, John	127	Stanfield, S.L.	187
Smith, J. R.	134	Stow, Albert	192
Skwortz, Mrs. S.	136	Stow, E. W.	192
Stephens, W. McD.	140	Stow, Able	192
Spears, J. B.	145	Stow, A. P.	192
Stahl, Daniel	147	Stow, Levi	193
Stahl, Julius	147	Stow, H. W.	193
Schneider, A. J.	148	Stow, Merritt	193
Schneider, Johann	148	Santos, Juan M. de los	194
Spiess, Hermann	149	Salinas, Anastacio	198
Schmitz, Jacob	149	Simpson, I. P.	198
Schmuck, Otto	151	Schurig, Adolph	199
Schafer, Philip	151	Smith, R. M.	201
Sailzer, Geo.	151	Smith, Joseph	201
Sahm, William	152	Serna, J. F.	205

INDEX.

NAMES.	PAGES.	NAMES.	PAGES.
Serna, P.	205	Smith, Joseph M.	271
Smith, T. A.	206	Sumners, A. M.	272
Smith, James jr.	210	Scrivner, D. D.	272
Schreier, Anton	212	Schorre, Julius	273
Schleyer, Christian	212	Schorlemmer, Wm.	274
Schleicher, G.	212	Spinks, Robert H.	275
Smith, James	218	Seitz, A.	277
Sampson, S.	220	Schiwetz, Jacob	280
Sittre, Jacob	223	Schiwetz, Fredk	280
Sittre, Joseph	223	Sager, Adam	281
Santleben, C. jr.	223	Seivers, A.	282
Santleben, C. sr.	223	Schafer, Chas.	283
Smith, James M. sr.	224	Stappe, James L.	284
Smith, Mrs. Lucinda	224	Sawyers, Miss F. L. M.	286
Stuckler, Wilhelm	225	Seay, Caspian	286
Seguin, Antonio	226	Stout, B. O.	287
Shely, John S.	227	Stoddard, Mrs. Jane	290
Smith, H. M.	229	Sawyer, Miss M. J.	290
Schmid, Martin	230	Sawyer, Mrs. Jane	290
Smith & Hale	231	Shaper, Henry	292
Stapper, Edward	233	Stewart, Joseph	294
Schulz, Carl	234	Sawyer, J. H.	294
Schnable, John	235	Sawyer, Miss A. T.	294
Schulz, Michael	235	Scott, C. P.	297
Schultz, J. H.	235	Stewart, J. G.	297
Schulz, Wm.	237	Sessions, S. M.	298
Schuler, Henry	229	Skloss, Adam	299
Schroub, Mrs. Sophia	239	Skloss, Anton	299
Schroub, Philip	239	Schefler, C.	300
Schneider, B.	240	Schefler, Frank	301
Sassmannhausen, Fred	241	Stephens, J. E.	305
Seiler, Wm.	241	Stillman, Chas. jr.	312
Seiler, Jacob	241	Swift, F. M.	316
Schneider, Christian	243	Shelly, Mrs. M.	316
Seiler, Miss Helena	243	Straugh, Anton	324
Saffold, Wm.	246	Skidmore, S. C.	326
Sasse, Louis	253	Stattler, V.	328
Strieber, Andrew	254	Simon, Conrad	329
Schuckler, John	256	Schafer, Ernest	331
Schneider, Daniel	256	Stucken, F. V. D.	332
Schaffe, Miss C.	257	Shaper, Mathias	332
Strieber, Adolph	258	Stendebach, I. F.	336
Stanchus, David	258	Stephen, Gotliebe	336
Sturmer, Gotliebe	259	Saner, Jacob	336
Sasse, Fredk	260	Staves, G.	337
Strieber, Chas.	261	Schlador, F. H.	338
Schultz, Gotliebe	263	Seidensticker, H.	338
Sickor, John	264	Serger, E.	338
Schley, Wm.	265	Schilling, E.	339
Sasse, Henry	267	Saur, F.	339

INDEX.

NAMES.	PAGES.	NAMES.	PAGES.
Schlador, C.	339	Stieler, G.	343
Saur, Henry	339	Smith, A. C.	347
Strohecker, L.	340	Scott, Jonathan	359
Schafer, Robt.	340	Scott, N. H.	259
Sennett, L. M.	342	Sikes, John	361
Sennett, Miss Amanda	342	Sikes, Mrs. M.	362
Schwethelm, E.	342	Smiley, N. M.	364
Schellhase, G.	343	Seale, E. F.	365
Schulze, F.	343	Swan, J. A.	367
Steeves, Robt.	343	Sommerville, S. E.	371
Taylor, James H.	10	Tollett, Wesley	124
Taylor, B. W.	16	Terry, C.	127
Taylor, T. E.	16	Terry, Nathaniel	127
Thomas, Ben.	18	Tarin, Juan	127
Thomas, Penelope	18	Tarin, Antonio	127
Thomas, Miss Laura J.	18	Tumlinson, Mrs. H.	129
Thomas, Benj. F.	18	Tumlinson, Miss S. J.	129
Thomas, Miss Penelope J.	18	Tumlinson, J. M. W.	129
Thomas, W. S.	19	Tumlinson, J. W.	129
Thompson, Mrs. Mary M.	19	Tumlinson, P. F.	129
Taschler, Mrs. Barb	26	Tumlinson, Joseph	129
Tschierhardt, Nicholas	30	Turner, C. S.	131
Turpe, John G.	30	Tournot L. H.	132
Tondre, Nicholas	39	Torrey, John F.	148
Tondre, Eugene	39	Trebes, John	150
Tomlin, W.	40	Trusch, Peter	150
Tomlin, A.	40	Twiefel, H.	155
Thien, John D.	42	Tolle, Fredrick	158
Tampke, Adolph	46	Tanner, S.	160
Tampke, Albert	53	Toller, J. T.	160
Tumlinson, T. C.	66	Tullos, R.	166
Tumlinson, C. M.	67	Taylor, Henry	169
Talk, A. W.	70	Truehart, J. L.	185
Talk, John	72	Taylor, P. C.	185
Tivy, J. A.	76	Twohig, John	185
Tyler, M. A.	81	Thompson, H. L.	187
Trabiaso, Manuel	84	Taylor, S. R.	192
Trabiaso, Melchor	84	Tegeda, Pedro	194
Tores, Miguil	84	Trevenio, Francisco	194
Trivino, L.	88	Toudouze, Gustava	195
Trivino, Pilar	88	Tynan, E.	203
Talamantes, Juan	93	Tores, Modest	206
Talamantes, Simon	94	Thompson, S. C.	212
Talamantes, Dario	95	Toole, E.	218
Turner, J. or agt.	99	Torrey, G. B.	220
Tyson, T. S.	106	Trimble, Edwin	221
Thresher, Mrs. M. P.	112	Trimble, Mrs. Mary	221
Tullos, Jas. M.	117	Trimble, J. G.	224
Tarin, Juan M.	123	Tarin, Joaquin	226

INDEX. 399

NAMES.	PAGES.
Trainer, J. M.	233
Thiele, Wm.	234
Tom, Dudley,	245
Tom, Wm.	245
Tom, Geo. A.	245
Tiner, J. F.	248
Taylor, Mrs. Elizabeth	250
Taylor, Miss E. J. & sisters	250
Taplor, W. B.	250
Taylor, Joseph	251
Taylor, John M.	251
Tumlinson, Joseph	253
Tumlinson, J. J.	253
Treude, John	262
Tumpke Ludolph	264
Tennille, Geo. C.	269
Taylor, Mrs. K. J.	270
Tuggle, T. J.	270
Tewes, Louis	274
Ubanzik, Mat.	73
Ulrich, George	153
Ulrich, Wm.	153
Uhr, Mathias	156
Uhr, H.	156
Uhr, Carl	159
Vanpelt, T. M.	9
Vance, John	29
Vollmer, Valentine	40
Vanpelt, G. G.	45
Vanpelt, G. G. & Bros.,	45
Vollrath, Louis	83
Valle Enseres del	84
Valdes, Josefa	87
Vogle, Louis	156
Voges, Diederich	160
Votaw, E.	165
Voges, Henrich	191
Valdes, F. Herrera de	197
Valdes, Francisco	197
Van Riper, G.	204
Wall, G. W.	9
Wall, D. D.	10
Westfall, E. D.	10
Watkins, T.	10
Ware, R. M.	17
Ware, Miss S. T.	17

NAMES.	PAGES.
Tennille Mrs. A. J.	275
Tennille, Mrs. S.	276
Trautwin, Wm.	281
Thieme, Mrs. C.	282
Thieme, G. L.	282
Taylor, Mrs. E. H.	283
Taylor, Josiah Estate of	283
Thigpen, John	285
Torain, W. B.	286
Torain, W. S.	286
Thompson, G. W.	292
Trivenia, U.	307
Townsend, S. L.	314
Timon, J.	326
Toomy, J. H.	326
Todd, G. W.	329
Taylor, H. M.	330
Trafton, M.	351
Talley, J. T.	364
Ujhazy, F.	183
Urbahn, Albert	209
Ucker, Wm.	214
Urban, C.	218
Urbann, John	300
Van Ward, Z.	207
Valdes, Salome	209
Vance, W.	212
Varga, Benj.	219
Vogt, Johan	229
Voges, Cord.	236
Vordenbaumen, Fredk.	242
Volkel, Geo.	266
Vogt, Adam	334
Vogt, August	335
Vanderstratten, F,	335
Vanderstratten, T.	336
Vogt, Rudolph	343
Vandergrift, Mrs. M. A.	350
Ware, John C.	17
Webster, Silas	17
Wright, Pleasant	19
Waclazyk, Frank	25
Wagner, Mrs. Caterina	26
Wernett, J. B.	27

INDEX.

NAMES.	PAGES.	NAMES.	PAGES.
Weber, August	32	West, J.	133
Weber, Joseph	33	West, David	133
Walter, Alois	36	West, Bud	133
White, Mrs. H.	41	Williams Joseph	134
Wantz, Mrs. Franciska	47	Williams, Wright	137
Wiemers, John H.	49	White, S. H.	139
Winkler, Nicholas	51	Williams, Mrs. Mary	140
Wiemers, C.	53	Woodward, J. G.	141
Wolf, Mrs. R.	54	Woodward, M.	141
Wolf, Jacob	54	Woodward, C.	141
Weynand, H.	56	Williams, Mrs. D. W.	145
Watkins, L. C.	60	Walzen, John	148
Williams, George	60	Wiskeman, Dan'l	150
Weston, John	64	Wolfshohl, August	150
Williams, Mrs. L.	66	Wengeroth, Mrs. Catherine	150
Wanzer & Teller	69	Wyel, John	151
Wishert, J. A.	70	Wahl, Philip J.	151
Wilburn, F. C.	72	Wenzel, Conrad	151
Wintrik, Lorenz	78	Wenzel, Ign.	154
Wilkinson, W. S.	82	Weilbacher, Jacob	155
Wheeler, David T.	83	Winkler, Miss Anna	157
Wheeler, J. E.	83	Wuest, Adam	158
Wayman, Mrs. E.	89	Wagner, Philip	158
Wright, Mrs. S. F.	98	Williams, J. R.	163
Williamson, Mrs. M.	99	Williams, W.	164
Wilson, J. P.	99	Williams, John	165
Watlon, D. A. T.	101	Waller, Henderson	166
Wilson, Jas. & J. E.	101	Williams, Henderson	168
Wilson, J. E, & J. P.	101	Wilburn, Thomas	169
Wilson, J. E.	101	Wright, G. W.	169
Williams, S. P. H.	101	Wilson, G. Z.	176
Williams, B. O. or agent	102	Wilson, Mrs. E. C.	176
Whitby, Mrs. P. or agent	102	Wimble, Caroline	178
Webster, N. C.	103	Walker, J. D.	178
Webster, David A.	103	Walker, S. W.	178
Wright, J. S.	105	Walker, W. C.	180
Winn, R. E., Est. of	103	Walker, A.	180
Williams, Henderson	109	Wadenpohl, John	183
Wilson, James	109	Wottley, Anton	186
Weed, John	113	Weir, James	186
Weed, Alfred	114	Ward, J. G.	191
Williams, Frank	119	White, Mary A.	196
Williams, L. D.	119	Werner, Christian	199
Walker, Joel M.	121	Weber, Joseph	200
Walker, Mrs. Emily	121	Weatherby, W. A.	201
Wieglendoz, Antonio	127	Wood, Mrs. J. C.	210
Winn, Mrs. C.	128	Walters, Mrs. Lucinda	218
Walker, Edward, or agent	128	Womble, S. S.	220
West, James	130	Wurzbach, F.	224
Ward, L. T.	133	Wurzbach, Adolph	225
West, G. W.	133	Wurzbach, Julius	226

NAMES.	PAGES.	NAMES.	PAGES.
Weir, Robt.	232	Wright, H. C.	311
Weyel, Aug.	235	Whelan, M.	315
Weidner, Henry	240	Williams, H. B.	317
Wetz, John	243	West, A. J.	319
Wilson, Joseph	245	West, B. F, Agt.	320, 321, 322
Walther, Charles	246	West, Michael	322
Williams, Ed. H.	246	Welder, T.	323
Wells, J. A.	248	Wood, J. H.	323
Ward, D. A.	249	Wagnon, J.	326
Woods, Mrs. Isabella	252	Whitehead, J.	326
Wright. L. B.	253	Williamson, J. M.	326
Willburn, Mrs. Phebe	255	Wright, Calvin	326
Westphal, Aug.	256	White, B. F.	327
Woods, H. G.	263	Wellington, R. ...	328
Wagenschein, Chas.	266	Williams, Louis	328
Wheat, Wm. M.	268	Weatherby, B. F.	329
Wofford, Webb	268	Wahrmund, E.	331
White, K. B.	270	White, Joseph	332
Wheat, Thos. J.	271	Weiss, A.	332
Webb, Mrs. C.	273	Weidenfeld, T.	338
Wheat, A. P.	274	Wittbold, Henry,	338
Webb, F. B.	275	Willie, H.	339
Wofford, Mrs. S. A.	275	Wilson, J. H.	345
Warren, Mrs. E.	275	Womach, E.	346
Winkler, Miss. T.	277	Wells, ... T. B.	347
Wrights, J. M.	285	Wright, H. C.	352
Williams, ... H.	285	Wright, L. C.	353
Wiltmer, Henry	291	Wilkinson, Miss. M. F.	355
Winslow, G.	292	White, C.	361
Williams, R.	299	Weber, H. J.	361
Wright, Sena	309	Wiley, S.	364
Wright, Joseph	310	Williams, Miss E.	364
Wright, C. F.	310	Webb, D. F.	367
Wright, Harriet	310	West, L. N.	368
Wright, T. C.	310	Weber, M.	370
Yeary, John	67	Yow, Mrs. C.	138
Yates, Mrs. Martha	69	Yarbrough, L. D.	177
Yozka, Frank	74	Yarbrough, A.	178
Yozka, Mary	74	Young, F. Xavera	224
Yoskula, Michael	79	Young, John	241
Yvaneo, Jose M.	89	Young, W. J.	241
Yndo, Miguel	97	Young, H. P.	243
Yelvington, H.	97	York, Jonathan	250
Young, Mrs. M.	108	Yocum, Jake	258
Yates, M. C.	135	Yocum, S. H.	260
Yates & Mansfield	135		
Zinsmiester, H.	26	Zerda, Nemencia de la	87
Zerner, Filip	78	Zerda, M. ne Jesus de la	88
Zerda, Ramon de la	86	Zaragoza, Mrs. C. F.	91

NAMES.	PAGES.	NAMES.	PAGES.
Zepada, Manuel	97	Zipp, John	234
Zepada, Jose	97	Zuhl, Fredk.	239
Zumwalt, T. B.	103	Zowada, Vincent	253
Zurcher, Nichola	154	Zimon, Walontina	260
Zuniga, Romano	197	Zuonn, Wilhelm	262
Zapada, Jesus	202	Zenerlc, F. J.	278
Zimili, Fritz	221	Zauner, Jocob	333
Zimili, Jacob	222	Zoeller, T.	335
Zuhl, Wm.	234	Zoeller, Adolph	337

French Merino Buck and Ewe, owned by W. A. Lockart, Bandera.

The Brand-Book Advertiser.

CHARLES HORN,
ENGRAVER,
SAN ANTONIO.

☞ All kinds of Seals, Stamps, &c. &c., made to order.

N. WINTHER,
GENERAL ENGRAVER,
SAN ANTONIO.

BOOK-BINDING.

The undersigned having established a Bindery in connection with the Herald Office, San Antonio, offers his services in every kind of Book-Binding, and promises to execute Work promptly and in a satisfactory manner, and would respectfully solicit a share of the public patronage.

WILLIAM SATTLER.

LINDMILLER & CO.,

WHOLESALE AND RETAIL DRUGGISTS AND GROCERS,

SAN ANTONIO,

Have taken the old stand of Dr. Lyons, on Commerce Street, near the Main Plaza, where they will keep always on hand

A FULL ASSORTMENT OF

Drugs, Medicines, Patent Medicines, Paints, Oils, Varnishes, Brushes, Perfumery, Fancy Articles, Flavoring Extracts, Spices, Fancy Groceries, Preserves, Jams, Jellies and Fruits, in Cans and Bottles.

ALSO—Pure French Brandy, Bourbon and Rye Whisky, Jamaica Rum and Holland Gin; Pure old Port, Sherry, Madeira and other Wines, and Ale and Porter, for Medical purposes—Together with every variety of Fancy Liquors, Cordials, and Syrups.

They will give particular attention to the sale of STAPLE DRUGS and PATENT MEDICINES. Also, to Preparations for the destruction of the SCREW WORM in Stock, and ask the attention of the Public to their STOCK CALOMEL and COMANCHE LINIMENT.

☞They have secured the services of Mr. JAMES CLAVIN, so long and favorably known in charge of the C. S. Hospital in San Antonio.

The old friends and customers of REED & Co. will also find J. P. REED with this firm.

☞ *All Articles sold by* LINDMILLER & CO., *are guaranteed* Pure *and* Fresh, *and will be sold as cheap or cheaper, than by any other Drug house in Western Texas.*

Buyers are respectfully requested to examine their Stock before purchasing elsewhere.

W. A. LOCKART.   W. C. RANDLE.

LOCKART & RANDLE,
WHOLESALE AND RETAIL GROCERS,
AND
COMMISSION MERCHANTS,

East side Main Plaza,

SAN ANTONIO.

Have on hand and are constantly receiving a fresh supply, by the quickest dispatch, of STAPLE AND FANCY GROCERIES, which are offered at the lowest Cash Prices the market can possibly afford—

—CONSISTING OF—

Sugars, Brown, Crushed, Loaf and Crushed Loaf; Coffee, Tea, Rice, Salt, Liverpool and Table; Tobacco, Segars, Whisky, Brandy, Holland Gin, Schnapps, Ale, Porter, Cordials, Wines, consisting of Clarets, White, Champagne, Cataba, Madeira, and Port; Blackberry and Ginger Wine; Cocktails, Whisky, Brandy and Gin; Plantation, Stomach, Grey and Red Jacket Bitters; Molasses and Golden Syrup; Canvass and Kentuky Hams; Bacon in Sides; Beef, Pickeled and Dried; Tongues, Pigs' Feet; Meats in Cans, of every variety, for the Traveling Public; Flour, Meal, Beans, Buckwheat, Macaroni, Vermecilla, Crackers, &c. Mackerel in whole, half, and quarter barrels and kits; Herrings, Salmon, Codfish, Sardines, Oysters, Lobsters, &c.; Candies and Fruits of every variety; Dried Peaches and Apples; Currants, Raisins, Cranberries, Can Fruits and Preserves of all kinds; Cheese, Western, Goshen and Pine Apple; Butter, Allspice, Ginger, Mace, Cinnamon, Nutmeg, Pepper, Black and Red. Mustard, Pickles of every variety; Yeast Powders, Soda, Condensed Milk and Concentrated Lye; Soaps, Candles, Star and Sperm. Oils, Linseed, Kerosene, Olive, Sweet and Salad; Turpentine, White Lead, Lamp Black, Varnishes, Copal and Black Leather; Hollow and Willow-Ware, consisting of Tubs, Buckets, Kegs, Market and Clothes Baskets, Clothes Pins and Lines, Brooms, Rope, Twins, Wool Baling, &c.: Dye-Stuffs, Copperas, Indigo, Madder, Venetian Red, Logwood. &c.

N. B. Hides and Pecans will be taken in exchange for Goods. A general supply of Sutler's Stores always on hand; and the patronage of Sutlers is respectfully solicited. Liberal deductions made to persons who buy to sell again.

THE BRAND-BOOK ADVERTISER.

Stock-Raisers, Farmers, Planters, Storekeepers, and Apothecaries!

TAKE NOTICE,

R. H. DRYDEN & Co.,

French's Building,

SAN ANTONIO,

KEEP on hand in quantities to suit purchasers, *and at the lowest rates, as they sell only for cash,*

Drugs and Medicines, Paints, Oils, Glass, Varnishes, Putty, Turpentine, Copperas, Alum, and Dye-Stuffs generally.

Fancy Articles and Perfumery,

THE CELEBRATED LONE STAR BAKING-POWDER—for baking light, sweet and nutricious BREAD—ready for baking as soon as mixed, and warranted to be made of the most simple and harmless materials; Corn Bread, Biscuit, Rolls, Buns, Puffs, and Batter-Cakes, may be prepared and cooked in *five minutes*—and the richness and delicacy of the article improved twenty-five per cent. It is made only by us.

We are the only authorized agents in Texas for the well known destroyer of that terror of Stock-raisers, the Screw-Worm,

BROWN'S YOUNG AMERICAN LINIMENT.

For Sprains, Old Swellings, Rheumatism, Callous Swellings, Indolent Tumors, Strains, Sprains, Bog Spavin, Sorebacks, Canker of the foot, Bad Thrushes, Itching Humors, Mange, Lice, &c., it cannot be excelled, and *for the Screw-Worm has never been equalled.*

DRYDEN & Co.

ARE the Proprietors of the following article, which they guarante equal to any thing of the kind ever invented, while it is sold 25 per cent cheaper:

DRYDEN'S
Compound Syrup of Wild Cherry,

For Coughs, Colds Croup, Asthma, Influenza, Hoarseness, Bronchitas, and the various affections of the Throat and Lungs.

Persons in the advanced stages of Consumption will experience relief. Children in Whooping Cough will be relieved by it if given in the intervals of the paroxysms.

The virtues of Wild Cherry have long been favorably esteemed in the treatment of the above diseases; and in offering this preparation to the afflicted, we are not presenting an untried or unknown thing. We prepare it daily from fresh materials and in a manner known only to ourselves—concentrate its virtues without dissipating the volatile and active ingredients on which its efficacy depends—combine with it valuable medicines whose virtues are recognized by all medical men, and pledge our word that relief will follow in all cases where administered according to the directions.

Prepared and sold only by
R. H. DRYDEN & CO.,
Apothecaries, French's Building, San Antonio.

☞ Orders sent in by your neighbors coming to town will be filled as honestly as though you come yourselves, and if you come yourselves call and see us and learn our prices, see our Goods, and then if you don't think it to your advantage to buy of us, we won't try to stop you from buying elsewhere.

R. H. DRYDEN & CO.,
French's Building, San Antonio.

6   THE BRAND-BOOK ADVERTISER.

C. K. RHODES.   GEO. S. DEATS.

RHODES & DEATS,

Manufacturers

OF

Copper, Tin,

AND

SHEET-IRON

WARE,

Dealers

IN

STOVES,

PUMPS,

Hollow ware,

Hardware,

AND

HOUSE-

FURNISHING

Goods,

Commerce Street, near Main Plaza,
SAN ANTONIO.

F. KALTEYER,
APOTHECARY, DRUGGIST & CHEMIST,

Presidio Street, near the Court-House,

SAN ANTONIO.

Keeps constantly on hand Fresh and Genuine Medicines, Domestic and Foreign, the latter by Direct Importation; to which he calls the particular attention of Country Practitioners, Planters, Farmers, and Stock-Raisers.

Medicine Chests and Homœpathic Medicines for family use.

Country Dealers supplied to their advantage with:

Patent Medicines. Perfumery, Oils, Turpentine, Sulphur, Saltpetre. Copperas, Blue Stone, Madder. Indigo, Black Lead, Rosin, &c.

F. KALTEYER'S SCREW-WORM LINIMENT,

Warranted to be at least equal to any Liniment recommended for that purpose, and *cheaper than any other.*

This Liniment not only destroys the Screw-Worm immediately, but heals the wound, and prevents the fly from blowing the wound again.

Good *Vinegar* manufactured constantly, and sold at the lowest market rates.

THE BRAND-BOOK ADVERTISER.

FRANK WEBB,
WM. POLK,
   New-Orleans,

JAMES ARBUCKLE,
A. G. DICKINSON,
   San Antonio.

WEBB, ARBUCKLE & CO.

General Commission Merchants,

AND

Wholesale and Retail Dealers in

Dry-Goods, Groceries, Hats, Caps,

Boots and Shoes,

SAN ANTONIO, TEX.

Solicit Consignments of Cotton, Wool, Hides, &c. &c. to their house in New-Orleans, upon which they will make liberal advances in both goods and money.

FRANK WEBB,
WM. POLK,
   New-Orleans.

JAMES ARBUCKLE,
A. G. DICKINSON,
   San Antonio.

WEBB, POLK & CO.,
COTTON FACTORS

AND

COMMISSION MERCHANTS,

NEW-ORLEANS, LA.

Offer their services to the Merchants and Planters of Texas, and will give prompt attention to Purchases and Sales. If most convenient, all settlements can be made with the San Antonio house. Particular attention given to Receiving and Forwarding Goods purchased in the Eastern markets.

J. F. CASIANO.   JOSE E. GARCIA.

CASIANO & GARCIA,
WHOLESALE AND RETAIL DEALERS
--IN--

Dry-Goods, Groceries, & General Merchandise,

West Side Main Plaza, adjoining Carolan's old Auction Stand,

San Antonio, Texas,

Ladies' and Gentlemen's Goods of every description, as well as Groceries, Liquors, and Wines, constantly arriving==all of which we propose to sell upon reasonable terms.

Purchasers will find at this house all of those leading articles usually kept in a Wholesale and Retail Dry=Goods and Grocery Store, to which we invite the attention of purchasers generally.

P. WAGNER.   F. RUMMEL.

WAGNER & RUMMEL,

Commerce street, near the Bridge,

SAN ANTONIO, TEXAS,

WHOLESALE AND RETAIL DEALERS

—IN—

Dry-Goods,	Hardware,
Clothing,	Cutlery,
Hats,	Crockery,
Shoes,	Groceries,
Hosiery,	Liquors,
Perfumery,	Tobacco,
Stationery,	Cigars, &c.

The only Agents in San Antonio for the Sale of the

COMAL MANUFACTURING COMPANY'S

SPUN COTTON AND DOMESTIC.

CASH paid for Country Produce.

MENGER HOTEL,
SAN ANTONIO, TEXAS.
W. A. MENGER, Proprietor.

A. J. RICE,
SADDLE AND HARNESS-MAKER,
KEEPS CONSTANTLY ON HAND
ALL VARIETIES OF SPANISH SADDLES, HARNESS,
SADDLERY HARDWARE, &c.
Commerce Street, San Antonio.

Particular attention paid to Sales of Real Estate, caballados of Horses,

AND

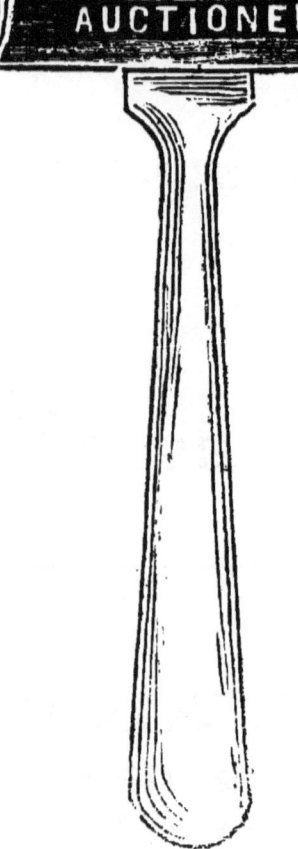

Trade-Sales of Merchandise.

☞ Can be consulted at the Menger Hotel.

MICHEL & CO.,
Commerce Street, San Antonio,

WHOLESALE AND RETAIL MERCHANTS,

Keep constantly on hand a large Stock of

Dry-Goods, Clothing, Boots, Shoes, Hats,

AND

A General Assortment of Groceries, Liquors, &c.

Will take Wool and Hides in exchange.

MICHEL & CO.

Valuable Improved Stock and Lands for Sale.

I offer for sale, for Cash, my Sheep Rancho in Bandera county, two miles East of the county town, and fronting on the Medina River, well improved and in good running order, containing 3,500 acres of Land, with 2000 head of Full Blood Merino and Grade Sheep upon it: (One hundred Full Blood Rams, fully guaranteed for breeding purposes, being on hand for sale, at any time called for;) together with all the fixtures and furniture necessary to carry it on successfully, including two dwelling houses, 1 cabin, field and pasture enclosed, corn, corn crib and stable, household furniture, horses, sheep and dogs, and within two miles of a Saw and Flouring Mill.

ALSO—the Estancia No. 2, four miles South of the former, upon Bruin Creek, containing 2000 acres of Land, connecting with valuable outlets for grazing purposes, with a cabin and good pens upon it, and watered by permanent springs at the Estancia, and bounded on the East by the Medina river. Both places have land upon them suitable for growing corn and wheat, and each place is desirable as a separate point for farming and stock-growing, and each can be purchased separately with part of the stock, or the stock purchased without the lands, as would suit a purchaser. I have also for sale several other Stock Ranchos, with the stock upon them, unimproved lands suitable for settlement, and irrigable Lots in San Antonio, for gardening purposes.

San Antonio, February 1, 1866.

JOHN JAMES.

The Sheep and the Rancho can be seen by applying to SAMUEL F. CHRISTIAN, Esq., on the premises, who will also sell the Bucks and give every information required.

DIRECT IMPORTATION.

Only one word!

H. GRENET,

Respectfully invites City and Country Merchants and the Public generally to examine his Stock before purchasing elsewhere.

By doing so they will find great inducement to their advantage.

Every Article is warranted as represented.

Liquors, Groceries, Crockery, Hardware, &c.

Dry Goods, Clothing, Hats, Boots, Shoes, &c.

E. M. SMITH.   HUGH F. YOUNG.

SMITH & YOUNG,

WHOLESALE GROCERS

AND

COMMISSION MERCHANTS,

Hospital Building, Solidad Street,

SAN ANTONIO.

WILL KEEP CONSTANTLY ON HAND A LARGE AND GENERAL STOCK

OF

Groceries and Provisions,

—ALSO—

WINES, BRANDIES,

AND

LIQUORS OF ALL DESCRIPTIONS.

☞ COUNTRY PRODUCE of all kinds taken in exchange or on commission.

Our motto is, *Small profits and quick Sales.*

COME AND SEE.

C. ROSSY.   C. F. VIERECK.   AUG. HARTMAN.

ROSSY, HARTMAN & CO.,

WHOLESALE DEALERS

IN

GENERAL MERCHANDISE,

—AND—

COMMISSION MERCHANTS,

Commerce Street,

SAN ANTONIO, TEXAS.

WOOL & HIDES

Bought at the highest market price.

Special attention given to all goods on consignment.

KLOCKENKEMPER & WINTHER,
WATCH-MAKERS, JEWELERS, & ENGRAVERS,
MAIN STREET, OPPOSITE KLOEPPER'S HOTEL,
SAN ANTONIO.
Repairing done to order, and all Work warranted.

BAR-ROOM AND FAMILY GROCERIES.

The undersigned have opened an establishment of the above character, to which they invite the attention of their friends and the public.

HUMPHREY & JOHNSON,
Alamo Plaza, 2d house North of Menger Hotel.

☞ There is also attached to the premises a wagon yard and horse lot, with all necessary conveniences.

MAUERMANN & KAPP,
Main Street, San Antonio, Texas,
Dealers in Guns, Pistols, and Sporting Materials.
REPAIRING done at short notice.

BELL & BROS.
DEALERS IN

Jewelry, Silver-ware, Plated-ware, Diamond Goods, American and European Watches and Clocks, Gold Pens and Pencils of every kind, Gold and Silver Thimbles, Gold, Silver, Steel and Tortoise-shell Spectacles and Eye-Glasses, with Pebble and Glass Lenses, suitable for the aged or near-sighted.

ENGRAVERS AND MANUFACTURERS OF ALL ARTICLES IN THEIR LINE.

☞ Watches, Clocks, and Jewelry, repaired and warranted.
☞ Orders filled promptly.

Main Street, five doors East of the Main Plaza,
(*Opposite their old Stand,*)
SAN ANTONIO, TEXAS.

C. UPSON,
Attorney and Counsellor at Law,
Office in Linn's Building, opposite Courthouse,
SAN ANTONIO, TEXAS.

TH. HERTZBERG.   FERD. SIMON.
HERTZBERG & SIMON,
Booksellers, Stationers, and Dealers
IN
Fancy Goods, Notions, Toys, etc.,
SAN ANTONIO, TEXAS.

F. W. SCHUNKE,
Dealer in Family Groceries
AND
GARDEN SEEDS,
MAIN STREET, NEXT DOOR TO DR. NETTE.

P. SHEINER,
Having removed to his new stand, South side Military Plaza, takes this occasion to inform the public that he is prepared to furnish them with almost everything usually kept in a

Dry-Goods, Grocery, or General Variety Store,

upon as reasonable terms as can be had at any other establishment in this market.

The highest market price paid for all kinds of saleable country Produce.

W. B. LEIGH,
LAWYER,
SAN ANTONIO.
(Office over Rhodes & Deats.)

CHA'S F. FISHER,
WATCHMAKER & JEWELER,
MAIN STREET, SAN ANTONIO,

Will be found at his old stand, ready and willing to repair Watches, Jewelry, &c., upon short notice and reasonable terms. None but the best Workmen employed, and all work warranted.

PURE FRENCH MERINO BUCKS,

For sale by W. A. Lockart, Bandera County,

Who can usually be found at the business house of Lockart & Randle, East side Main Plaza, San Antonio.

THO'S JOHNSON.   F. McC. NEWTON.

JOHNSON & NEWTON,
DEALERS IN
STAPLE & FANCY GROCERIES,

North-East corner Main Plaza, San Antonio.

Where will be found at all times, and at reasonable rates,

FAMILY SUPPLIES,

And every thing called for in the Grocery line, both at Wholesale and Retail, and where fair prices will be paid for all kinds of Country Produce.

GEORGE HOERNER'S

BAR-ROOM,

Main Street, San Antonio,

Has the very best of Liquors, Wines, Cigars, &c., where those who derive pleasure from the "O be joyful," will find comfort and consolation.

GREAT FURNITURE HOUSE.

WM. CHRYSLER,

South-East Corner Main Plaza,
SAN ANTONIO, TEXAS.

Is constantly receiving from the Northern and Western Markets,

THE LATEST AND MOST ELEGANT STYLES OF

FURNITURE

—CONSISTING OF—

Rosewood, Walnut, Mahogany, & Enameled Chamber Suits,

Sofas, Bureaus, Wardrobes, Tables, Chairs, Bedsteads, &c.

ALSO

Wire and Tin Safes, of every variety.

—TOGETHER WITH—

DRY GOODS, FANCY GOODS,
CROCKERY, TOYS, &c.

☞ All of which he offers at the lowest market prices.

WOOL & HIDES
Bought at the highest market price.

C. E. JEFFERSON.   H. L. RADAZ.   JULIEN FIELD.

JEFFERSON, RADAZ & CO.,
AUCTIONEERS
AND
COMMERCIAL BROKERS.

AUCTION DAYS:
MONDAYS, WEDNESDAYS & SATURDAYS.

We are in receipt of regular supplies of Staple Goods for AUCTION SALES.

AT PRIVATE SALE:

We have on hand a large assortment of GROCERIES, LIQUORS, and FAMILY SUPPLIES, generally, and will be "*re-inforced*" regularly and speedily.

REAL ESTATE.

From the long residence of two of our firm, and their experience and knowledge of the records, we are prepared to buy and sell Real Etate to the best advantage.

First Monday in every Month
Set apart for Sales of Real Estate at Auction.

We have a safe enclosure for Carriages, Buggies, &c.

Promptness can be relied on in all our transactions.

Liberal Advances made on Consignments.

LONE STAR DRUG STORE.

DR. W. D. EASTLAND,
On Main Street, East of the Bridge, San Antonio.

PHYSICIANS,	STOCKRAISERS,
MERCHANTS,	FARMERS,
PLANTERS,	FAMILIES,

Can have their wants supplied in a satisfactory manner. I study to please, and try to act on the square.

DRUGS & MEDICINES, PAINTS & OILS, FANCY SOAPS & PERFUMERY, COMBS & BRUSHES, FRUITS & JELLIES, FANCY GROCERIES AND **PATENT MEDICINES**

Constantly on hand and frequently arriving, fresh and genuine. No credit. *That* has been my ruin once.

Sashes, Doors, and Blinds,
Made to order at their Factory at New Braunfels.
KOESTER & TOLLE.

WOOLCARDING
Done at the Factory of
KOESTER & TOLLE,
New-Braunfels.

ELSKES & CO.,

Guilbeau Building,

WEST OF THE SAN PEDRO,

SAN ANTONIO.

PROVISION STORE.

Window Glass--all sizes.
Oils, Paints, Turpentine,
Brushes, Pencils,
Carpenter's Tools.

Commission and Storage.

Cash paid for Country Produce.

THE SAN ANTONIO LEDGER:

A WEEKLY AND TRI-WEEKLY NEWSPAPER.

Published in San Antonio, Texas.

J. M. MORPHIS, Editor.   **J. M. SMITH, Publisher.**

Terms:

Weekly, per annum, $6 00 Currency,
"   "   six months,   3 00   "
Tri-Weekly, per annum,   12 00   "
"   "   six months,   6 00   "

Job Work, plain or ornamental, of every variety, such as Posters, Blanks, Pamphlets, Bill-heads, Cards, &c., done at the shortest notice.

JOB PRINTING OFFICE

OF THE

SAN ANTONIO "EXPRESS" AND "FREE PRESS."

The undersigned, having a fine assortment of PRINTING MATERIAL, including Plain & Ornamental Type, of every variety, would respectfully solicit the patronage of the citizens of San Antonio, and the community generally, who have any business in this line, and they may be assured that it will be attended to with neatness and dispatch.

JOB WORK

In-English, Spanish, French and German,

—SUCH AS—

Posters,   Handbills,   Programmes,
Catalogues,   Pamphlets,   Cards, &c.,

Executed at the shortest notice.

"THE FREE PRESS," a German paper, having the largest circulation of any paper in Western Texas, offers its advertising columns to the public in general at liberal terms. Circulation 1200. No extra charge for translating.

E. PENTENRIEDER,

SAN ANTONIO,

WHOLESALE AND RETAIL DEALER

—IN—

FANCY GOODS AND NOTIONS,

STATIONERY,

CUTLERY, GLASS AND CHINA

WARE,

PERFUMERY,

Musical Instruments,

Looking-Glasses, Picture-Frames,

Window-Glass, &c.

E. MARUCHEAU.   C. MARUCHEAU.

E. MARUCHEAU & Co.,
COMMISSION MERCHANTS
AND
DEALERS IN DOMESTIC AND FOREIGN
DRY-GOODS.
CLOTHING, HATS, BOOTS AND SHOES,
Crockery, Groceries, Wines and Liquors, &c.
WHOLESALE AND RETAIL,
COMMERCE STREET, SAN ANTONIO, TEXAS.

C. MARUCHEAU.   E. G. DE L'ISLE, Jr.

MARUCHEAU & DE L'ISLE,
Importers and Wholesale Dealers
IN
FRENCH AND STAPLE DRY-GOODS,
Wines, Brandies, &c.
AND
COMMISSION MERCHANTS,
STRAND, GALVESTON.

Being well represented in New-York and New-Orleans, we can with security offer our services to our friends and the public in general.

ALL CONSIGNMENTS and ORDERS to either our firm at Galveston or San Antonio, will receive our greatest attention, and no efforts will be spared to give entire satisfaction.

P. C. TAYLOR,

(AT THE OLD MARTIN STAND)

KEEPS CONSTANTLY ON HAND

A good supply of all kinds of

GENERAL MERCHANDISE

———o———

Here you will find every thing that you require, at the lowest living rates, and every thing guaranteed as represented.

The highest market price

PAID FOR COUNTRY PRODUCE.

I only ask that you call and see me before purchasing elsewhere.

Free yardage connected with the Store.

FIRST PREMIUM
IMPROVED
$10 SEWING MACHINE. $10

THE EMBODIMENT OF PRACTICAL UTILITY AND EXTREME SIMPLICITY.

Originally patented May 13, 1862—improvement patented June 9, 1863. The celebrated FAMILY GEM SEWING MACHINE, with CRIMPING attachment—a most Wonderful and Elegantly Constructed Novelty; is noiseless in operation, uses the straight Needle, and works horizontal, sews with Double or single Thread of all kinds; makes the stitch *more perfect* and *regular* than by hand, and with extraordinary rapidity, making 16 stitches to the evolution of the wheel. Will *Gather, Hem, Ruffle, Shirr, Tuck, Run up Breadths, &c., &c.*; requires no *Change of Stitch*—IS NOT LIABLE TO GET OUT OF ORDER, and will last a LIFETIME; being the strongest machine made. *Warranted* not to get out of order for THREE YEARS. It has taken the PREMIUMS at New York and other STATE FAIRS, and received the FULL APPROVAL OF ALL the *principal Journals*, and of those who have USED THEM.

"This beautifull Machine makes the Running Stitch at the rate of several yards per minute.—Frank Leslie.

"It uses a common needle, sews very rapidly, and is so easily understood that a child can use it.—N. Y. Independent.

"With single or double thread, it silently yet very rapidly, with a common needle, makes the running stitch exactly like hand sewing.—N. Y. Tribune.

☞ Single Machines sent to any part of the country per Express, packed in box with printed instructions, on receipt of price, $10.

Safe delivery guaranteed.

Agents wanted everywhere. Circular, containing liberal inducements, sent free.

Address all orders to   **ED. H. QUICK,**
Sole Agent for Texas,
At Bryant's News Depot, Houston, Tex.

J. EISEMAN.   E. ROTHSCHILD.

EISEMAN & ROTHSCHILD,

Main Street, San Antonio,

WHOLESALE AND RETAIL DEALERS

—IN—

DRY-GOODS,

Ready-made Clothing, Casimeres and Tailors' Findings, Boots, Shoes, Hats, Caps, Leather and Shoe Findings. Tobacco & Cigars.

......

The highest cash price paid for Wool, Hides and Pecans.

Purchasers will find it to their interest to give us a call before purchasing elsewhere.

C. MONOD,

Vances' Stores, Alamo Plaza,

SAN ANTONIO,

COMMISSION AND FORWARDING

MERCHANT,

AND

DEALER IN

DRY-GOODS,

GROCERIES,

HARDWARE,

&c.   &c.   &c.

F. A. SEFFEL.   PHIL. SHARDEIN,
Formerly of the firm of Marshal & Bro.

SEFFEL & SHARDEIN,

Commerce Street, near the old Bridge,
SAN ANTONIO,

Wholesale and Retail Dealers in

STOVES,

TIN, SHEET-IRON & COPPER WARE, &c.

Having several years experience in the above line, they feel confident of giving satisfaction to those favoring them with their patronage.

Country Merchants and purchasers generally are requested to give them a call before purchasing elsewhere.

FRANK RADAZ,

Solidad street, opposite the Veremendi House,
SAN ANTONIO.

Is constantly receiving and keeps on hand

A GENERAL ASSORTMENT OF

FAMILY AND FANCY GROCERIES

Of the very best quality,

Which he offers at reasonable prices.

☞ All kinds of Country praduce bought and sold, and persons visiting the city with such articles to dispose of, will please give him a call and examine his stock before making their purchases at other establishments.

FRANK & SICHEL,

—AT—

Devine's Old Stand, Main Plaza,

SAN ANTONIO,

WHOLESALE AND RETAIL DEALERS

—IN—

Staple & Fancy Dry Goods,

BOOTS, SHOES & HATS,

CLOTHING AND GENTLEMEN'S FURNISHING GOODS,

Staple & Fancy Groceries,

TOBACCO & SEGARS,

CROCKERY GLASS, AND WOODEN WARE,

Stationery, Notions, &c.

We particularly invite Planters and Stockraisers to call at our well known Store, front of the Main Plaza, where all kinds of Country Produce will be taken in exchange for Goods.

FRANK & SICHEL.

NORTON & BROS.,

Main Plaza,

SAN ANTONIO, TEXAS,

DEALERS IN

Hardware, Cutlery, Wooden-ware, Tin-Plate, Sheet-Iron, Nails, Paints, Oils, Glass,

SADDLERY, SADDLERS' FINDINGS, &c.

Also,
DEALERS IN
Pure Liquors & Cigars.

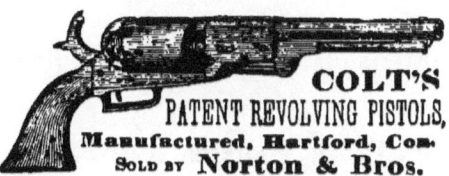

COLT'S PATENT REVOLVING PISTOLS,
Manufactured, Hartford, Con.
SOLD BY **Norton & Bros.**

Who have a large assortment constantly on hand at their

HARDWARE STORE,
Main Plaza, San Antonio.

GONZALES & Co.,

French's Building,

SAN ANTONIO, TEXAS,

AND

SAN LUIS POTOSI, MEX.

Dealers in General Merchandise,

AND

COMMISSION MERCHANTS.

Prompt attention given to collections against parties in Mexico.

Wool, Hides, Peltries and Pecans,
Bought at the highest market price.

Special attention given to Goods on consignment.

Having superior accommodations for storage, we are prepared to receive and store Goods at the usual rates.

WESTERN BREWERY

SAN ANTONIO, TEXAS.

W. A. MENGER, Proprietor.

The San Antonio Herald,

A DAILY AND WEEKLY NEWSPAPER.

J. D. LOGAN & G. H. SWEET, Proprietors.

Subscription to DAILY, $16 (currency) per year in advance.
" " WEEKLY, 5 " " " " "

Job Work and advertising done at the lowest rates.

HALFF & LEVY,

WHOLESALE AND RETAIL DEALERS IN

Fancy and Staple Dry Goods,

Clothing, Hats, Boots and Shoes,

Commerce Street,

SAN ANTONIO.

Strict attention paid to orders from Country Dealers.

Highest Cash prices paid for HIDES.

J. MARIA GARCIA VILLAREAL,
Wholesale and Retail Dealer in
DRY-GOODS AND GROCERIES,

Three doors below Mr. Morris Commerce St., San Antonio.

☞ The old friends of NARCISO LEAL will find him at this establishment.

J. M. MORPHIS,
LAWYER,
SAN ANTONIO.

(LEDGER OFFICE.)

GILBERT B. HATHAWAY

Begs leave to inform the citizens of San Antonio and vicinity, that he has recently opened a

WHOLESALE & RETAIL GROCERY STORE,

On Commerce Street, 2d door below Louis Zork, where he will sell all articles in his line for the lowest cash prices.

☞ Goods consigned to him will be sold for moderate commissions.

JS. DRESEL.   L. BRIAM.

DRESEL & BRIAM,

Main Street, San Antonio,

WHOLESALE AND RETAIL DEALERS

—IN—

GROCERIES AND DRY-GOODS,

Tobacco, Liquors & Wines, Shoes, Hats, Crockery,

And General Merchandise particularly well assorted to meet the wants of the Farming Community.

LOVENSTEIN & Co.,

At Post's old Stand Commerce Street,

SAN ANTONIO, TEXAS,

Wholesale and Retail Dealers

—IN—

DRY-GOODS, CLOTHING,

FANCY GOODS, GENTLEMEN'S FURNISHING GOODS,

Also, a large assortment of

HATS, BOOTS, SHOES, &c.

A. MORRIS,

WHOLESALE AND RETAIL DEALER

—IN—

Fancy Dry-Goods,

Clothing, Hats, Boots, Shoes,

AND

GROCERIES,

Commerce street,
SAN ANTONIO.

BAYLESS, BELL & Co.

Grocers, Commission Merchants,

And Dealers in Foreign and Domestic Liquors,
Main Street, opposite Foot Bridge, San Antonio, Tex.

T. COPELAND,

Manufacturer of

GINGER-POP & SPRUCE BEER,

SAN ANTONIO, TEX.

Always a few hundred dozen empty Bottles on hand and for sale.

ROBT. W. KEYWORTH,

General Agent and Collector,

Office on Presidio street, between Flores and Acequia sts.,
SAN ANTONIO, TEXAS.

Land, Lots, Horses, and Stock Cattle for sale.

S. E. JAQUA.   J. G. FAIDLEY.

JAQUA & FAIDLEY,

Sign of the "Big Boot," Commerce St., near Main Plaza, San Antonio,

Dealers in Boots, Shoes and Hats.

JOHN VANCE,
CASTROVILLE,

Has re-opened his Store, and will receive constant additions direct from New York and New Orleans to his present stock of

Hardware, Cutlery, Willow-ware, Groceries, Crockery, Tin-ware, Furniture, Dry-Goods, Hats, Boots and Shoes, Patent Medicines, Dried and Can Fruits, &c. &c.

He will pay Cash for Country Produce, such as Corn, Wheat, Dried Beef-Hides, Dressed Deer Skins, Sheep and Goat Skins, Bacon, Lard, Beeswax, Honey, Pecans, &c.

M. CASTANOLA,

Carata Street, San Antonio,

Will be found at his old stand, dealing as formerly in Groceries, Confectionaries, and Family Supplies generally.

B. OPPENHEIMER & CO.,
DEALERS IN

Staple and Fancy Dry-Goods, Boots, Shoes, Clothing, Hats,
&c. &c.

Opposite Foot Bridge, Main Street, San Antonio.

E. RICHTER,
Bar-Room and Beer Saloon,

At the Old Stand near Hummel's,

SAN ANTONIO, TEX.

HERM. IKEN,
Commission & Forwarding Merchant,
INDIANOLA, TEX.

C. L. PROBANT,
SAN ANTONIO,
Wholesale and Retail Dealer in General Merchandise,

F. UMSCHEID,
BAR-ROOM AND BEER-SALOON,
East side Military Plaza,
SAN ANTONIO.

D. RUSSI,
Beer-Saloon and Bar-Room,
North-East corner Military Plaza, San Antonio.

STURM & WEBER,
Bar-Room and Beer-Saloon,
South end Veremendi Building,
SAN ANTONIO, TEX.

I. P. SIMPSON.
LAWYER,
SAN ANTONIO, TEX.

Office, French's Building.

WM. W. GAMBLE,

GENERAL DEALER IN

BOOKS, STATIONERY AND NOTIONS,

Main Plaza, next door to the Post Office,

SAN ANTONIO, TEXAS.

An assortment of Literature, consisting in part of English, French and American Publications, School Books, Engravings, Lithographs, &c. &c. constantly on hand.

Subscriptions taken for the principal Newspapers and Periodicals published in this country.

J. G. BOOTH.   F. W. SIBERT.

BOOTH & SIBERT,
Auctioneers and Commission Merchants,
Main Plaza, San Antonio,

Have secured and are in possession of the Old Auction Stand for so many years occupied by the late JOHN CAROLAN, and which is also known as being visited by a larger number of purchasers than any other Auction stand in the city, in consequence of its locality being peculiarly well adapted to the

AUCTION BUSINESS.

Persons having any thing whatever to dispose of at auction will do well to place it with us, as we always have a large audience and liberal bidders.

SIMON MENGER,
SOAP & CANDLE MANUFACTURER,
Laredo Street, West of the San Pedro,
SAN ANTONIO, TEXAS.

JOHN KIRKPATRICK,
DEALER IN
Dry-Goods, Staple and Fancy Groceries, Boots, Shoes, Hats, and country Produce.

East side San Antonio River, near Mill Bridge, where you will find the clever and obliging T. H. BARRY, of the Texas Ranger

---

Z. VAN WARD,
Corner of Flores street and Military Plaza,

SAN ANTONIO,

GROCER AND PRODUCE MERCHANT,

C. MUNZENBERGER, CLERK.

Will attend to all consignments of Produce from the country.

Particular attention given to Beef Hides and Peltry.

Liberal advanes made on all consignments.

Orders from the country promptly attended to.

A. NETTE

Has just received direct from Europe, and selected by him= self for this market, a large stock of

Drugs, Medicines, Perfumeries, and Surgical Instruments.

All of those leading articles, such as Patent Medicines, &c. &c., usually kept in a first-class Drug Store, will be found at this establishment.

GOLDFRANK, FRANK & CO.,

SUCCESSORS TO

LAVANBURG & BRO.,

Main Street, San Antonio, Texas.

IMPORTERS

AND

WHOLESALE DEALERS

—IN—

FOREIGN & DOMESTIC
DRY-GOODS,

ALSO,

BOOTS, SHOES AND HATS.

N. C. LEROUX. N. J. COSGROVE.

LEROUX & COSGROVE,

Commerce Street, San Antonio,

MANUFACTURERS

OF

TIN, SHEET-IRON AND COPPER

WARE,

AND DEALERS IN

STOVES, PUMPS, &c.

Having the largest establishment of the above character in Western Texas, and being determined not to allow others to surpass us in accommodations and cheapness of Goods, we invite dealers to call at our store, examine wares, and ask prices.

TIN-ROOFING and Repairing done at the shortest notice and upon reasonable terms.

HUMMEL & BERENDS,
COMMERCE STREET, SAN ANTONIO,
DEALERS IN BOOKS, STATIONERY, FINE CUTLERY, FANCY ARTICLES, AND NEWS AGENTS.

COLT'S PATENT FIRE ARMS MAN'F'G CO.,
HARTFORD, CONN.

Have also on hand a fine assortment of Double Barrel Guns, Rifles, Colt's and other make of Pistols, paper and metal Cartridges for Rifles and Pistols, Ely's double Water=Proof Caps, Shot=pouches and Belts, fine and common assorted sizes Powder=Flasks, &c. &c.

BENJ. THOMAS. THOS. R. STEWART.

THOMAS & STEWART,
North-West corner Main Plaza and Acequia street,
SAN ANTONIO,

DEALERS IN DRY-GOODS, GROCERIES, COUNTRY PRODUCE, &c. &c.

In fact, almost every thing coming under the head of Family Supplies, may be found at this Store, and sold upon as reasonable terms as they can be had at any other establishment in the City.

Give us a call, and be convinced that what we tell you is no 'joke.'

HENRY LAAGER'S
Bar-Room and Beer-Saloon,
Veremendi Building, San Antonio.

Has been renovated, refitted and replenished. Clean Glasses, the best of Liquors, and polite bar-tenders, will be found at this establishment.

TOM KENNEDY'S
BAR-ROOM,
Carcel street, opposite the market-house.

Has on hand the best Brandies, Whiskeys, Gin, Sherry, Claret, Port and Champagne Wines, Absynth, Bitters, &c. &c. Also, the best brands
Cigars and Tobacco.

JOHN M. CAMPBELL,
BUILDER,

Having returned to San Antonio after an absence of four years, takes this method of returning thanks to his friends and fellow-citizens generally, for the kindness heretofore extended to him, and hopes by strict attention to business, good workmanship, &c., &c., to merit a liberal share of their patronage.

JOHN EARL'S SALOON,
Corner Main Plaza and Solidad St., San Antonio.

Wines, Brandies, Scotch, Irish, Old Monongahela and Bourbon Whisky, Lager-Beer, Fancy Liquors, &c.

A. VARGA,
Saddle and Harness Maker,
A few doors below L. Zork's, San Antonio, Tex.

Keeps constantly on hand Saddles, Bridles, Harness, Saddle-Bags, &c., in fact, all of those articles usually kept in a well-regulated Shop—all of which are made of the very best material, and in the most substantial manner—Cheap for cash.

HENRY BORCHERS,
New Fountain, Medina County, Tex.
Retail Dealer in Dry-Goods, Groceries & Family Supplies.

The weary traveler will also find at this establishment something to enliven and invigorate, if the very best old 'Rye' and 'Bourbon' will have that effect.

FIELD, EAGAR & CO.,

GENERAL MERCHANDISE

Shippers of and Dealers in

Hides, Wool and Pecans,

Masonic Hall Building,

SAN ANTONIO, TEXAS.

W. A. BENNETT,

Banker, Dealer in Exchange and Government

SECURITIES,

SAN ANTONIO, TEXAS.

☞ Will pay particular attention to the Collection of Claims at all accessible points in Texas.

J. H. FRENCH.   J. F. MINTER.   H. B. ADAMS.

J. H. FRENCH & CO.,

Commission and Exchange Brokers,

San Antonio, Texas.

☞ Prompt attention given to the Collection of Claims.

ESTRAYS.

[Brand: J in box]

During the past few years, I have had several horses taken from me (generally after the hour that an honest and God-loving man would be supposed to have said his prayers and retired to his peaceful couch) —all being branded as in the margin.

Never having sold or donated a horse wearing the above brand, I claim them as my property, wherever they may be found, and will largely thank and liberally reward any person who will assist me in recovering animals as mysteriously 'spirited' away. W. H. JACKSON, San Antonio.

[Brand: JP]

The owner of the brand given in the margin, whoever he or she may be, can learn something of much pecuniary advantage by addressing
LONG & JACKSON,
San Antonio.

[Brands: ?J and JP and TJ2]

Estrayed or stolen from the undersigned the following horses: One a bay, 5 or 6 years old, branded on left shoulder as in left margin, has a small scar on left side of neck; another, a bay, 10 years old, branded on left shoulder as in right margin; also, one sorrel horse, 7 years old, blaze face, some white feet, and branded on left shoulder as in opposite margin.

[Brands: AB and JB]

Any information leading to the recovery of the above described horses, or either one of them, will be thankfully received, and the informant liberally rewarded by
N. M. C. PATTERSON, Sabinal, Uvalde Co.

[Brands: JA and P and JK]

Strayed or stolen from the undersigned, one dark bay mare, 7 years old, some white in the face, and branded on shoulder as in left margin. Also, one young sorrel horse with some white in the face, also some white feet, and branded as in the right margin. Any one giving information leading to the recovery of either or both of the above animals, will be liberally rewarded by
Mrs. ANN L. HARPER,
New Fountain, Medina Co.

MASONIC.

THE GRAND LODGE OF THE STATE OF TEXAS,

Meets permanently in the city of Houston, on the second Monday of June, every year. The other grand bodies meet at the same time and place.

HOLLAND LODGE No. 1.—Held at the city of Houston on the second and fourth Monday in each month.

WASHINGTON CHAPTER No. 2—Held at the city of Houston, on the first Monday in each month.

AUSTIN LODGE No. 12—Held at the city of Austin, on the second Monday in each month.

LONE STAR CHAPTER No. 6—Held at the city of Austin, on the second Saturday in each month.

HARMONY LODGE No. 6—Held in the city of Galveston on the first and third Mondays in each month.

SAN FILLIPE DE AUSTIN CHAPTER No. 1—Held at the city of Galveston, on the first Tuesday in each month.

GONZALES LODGE No. 30—Held at Gonzales in the County of Gonzales on the first Saturday in each month.

GONZALES CHAPTER No. 51—Held at Gonzales in the county of Gonzales on the Friday of or immediately preceeding the full moon in each month.

ALAMO LODGE No. 44—Held at San Antonio in the County of Bexar, on the first Saturday in each month.

BURLESON CHAPTER No. 21—Held at San Antinio in the County of Bexar on the second Saturday of each month.

GOLIAD LODGE No. 94—Held at Goliad, in the County of Goliad, on the first Saturday in each month.

GOLIAD CHAPTER No. 54—Held at Goliad in the County of Goliad on the third Saturday in each month.

GUADALUPE LODGE No. 109—Held at Seguin in the County of Guodalupe on the first Monday of each month.

KEYSTONE CHAPTER No. 56—Held at Seguin in the County of Guadalupe on Sat- preceeding the first Monday in each month.

INDIANOLA LODGE No. 84—Held at Indianola, in the County of Calhoun on the second Wednesday in each month.

INDIANOIA CHAPTER No. 35—Held at Indianola in the County of Calhoun on the second Saturday in each month.

LAVACA LODGE No. 36—Held at Port Lavaca in the County of Calhoun on the first and third Saturday of each month.

CAMERON LODGE No. 76—Held in the Town of Clinton, in the County of DeWitt on the third Saturday in each month.

COLETTE LODGE No. 124—Held at Yorktown in the County of DeWitt, on the second Saturday in each month.

BELMONT LODGE No. 131—Held at Belmont in the County of Gonzales on the third Saturday in each month.

CONCRETE LODGE No. 182—Held at Concrete in the County of DeWitt, on the first Saturday of each month.

HOPKINSVILLE LODGE No. 183—Held at Hopkinsville, in the County of Gonzal- es, on the third Saturday of each month.

CORPUS CHRISTI LODGE No. 189—Held at Corpus Christi, in the County of Nu- eces, on the first Monday in each month.

REFUGIO LODGE No. 190—Held at Refugio in the County of Refugio on the sec- ond Saturday in each month.

DEMOLAY LOEGE No. 199—Held at Sandies Chapel, in the County of Gonzales on the second Saturday of each month.

BRAHAN LODGE No. 226—Held at Bethsada, in the County of Guadalupe on the Saturday on or before the full moon of each month.

BLACK POINT LODGE No. 250—Held at St. Marys, in the County of Refugio, on the Saturday of or before the full moon of each month.

HONDO LODGE No. 252—Held at Hondo Valley, in the County of Medina, on the second Saturday in each month.

BEEVILLE LODGE No. 261—Held in Beeville, County of Bee, on the third Sat- urday of each month.

COMAL LODGE 276—Held at New Braunfels, in the County of Comal on the Sat- urday of or after the full moon in each month.

PLEASANTON LODGE U. D. Held at Pleasanton, in the County of Atascosa, on the last Saturday in each month.

RIO GRANDE LODGE No. 81—Held at the city of Brownsville in the County of Cameron, on the first and third Saturdays in each month.

INDEX TO ADVERTISEMENTS.

NAMES.	PAGE
Bell & Bro.	17
Bayless, Bell & Co.	38
Bennett, W. A.	47
Borchers, Henry	46
Cassiano & Garcia	9
Chrysler, Wm.	20
Copeland, T.	38
Castanola, M.	39
Campbell, John M.	46
Dryden, R. H. & Co.	4 & 5
Dresel & Briam	37
Eastland, Dr. W. D.	22
Elskes & Co.	23
Eiseman & Rothschild	29
Earl, John	46
Fisher Chas. F.	19
Frank & Sichel	32
French, J. H. & Co.	47
Field, Eagar & Co.	47
Grenet H.	14
Gonzalez & Co.	34
Gamble, W. W.	41
Goldfrank, Frank & Co.	43
Horn, Charles	1
Humphrey & Johnson	17
Hertzberg & Simon	18
Hoerner, George	19
Halff & Levy	36
Hathaway, Gilbert B.	36
Hummel & Berenda	45
Iken, Herm.	40
James, John	13
Johnson & Newton	19
Jefferson, Radaz & Co.	21
Jaqua & Faidley	39
Kaltoyer, F.	7
Klockenkemper & Winther	17
Koester & Tolle	22
Keyworth, Robt. W.	38
Kirkpatrick, John	42
Kennedy, Tom	46
Lindmiller & Co.	2
Lockart & Randle	8
Leigh, W. B.	18

NAMES.	PAGES.
Lockart, W. A.	19
Ledger Newspaper	24
Lovenstein & Co.	37
Leroux & Cosgrove	44
Laager, Henry	46
Menger, W. A.	11 & 35
Michel & Co.	13
Mauermann & Kappe	17
Marucheau & Co.	26
Marucheau & De L'Isle	26
Monod C.	30
Morphis, J. M.	36
Morris, A.	38
Menger, Simon	41
Norton & Bros.	38
Nette, A.	42
Oppenheimer & Co.	39
Pentenreider, E.	25
Probant, C. L.	40
Quick, Ed. H.	28
Rhodes & Deats	6
Rice, A. J.	11
Robinson, J. D.	12
Rossy, Hartman & Co	16
Radaz, Frank	31
Richter, E.	39
Russi, D.	40
Smith & Young	15
Schunke, F. W.	18
Scheiner, P.	18
Seffel & Shardein	31
Sturm & Weber	40
Simpson, I. P.	40
Taylor, P. C.	27
Thomas & Stewart	45
Upson, C.	18
Umscheid, F.	40
Villareal, J. Maria Garcia	36
Vance, John	39
Van Ward, Z.	42
Varga, A.	46
Winther, N.	1
Webb, Arbuckle & Co.	8
Wagner & Rummel	10

www.ingramcontent.com/pod-product-compliance
Lightning Source LLC
Chambersburg PA
CBHW031153020526
44117CB00042B/962